BOBBY
MOORE

BOBBY
MOORE

By The Person Who Knew Him Best

TINA MOORE

CollinsWillow

An Imprint of HarperCollins*Publishers*

First published in UK in 2005 by
CollinsWillow
an imprint of HarperCollins*Publishers*
London

1

A CIP catalogue record for this book is
available from the British Library

ISBN 0 00 717396 2

Set in 12/17 pt Linotype Sabon by
Rowland Phototypesetting Ltd, Bury St Edmunds, Suffolk

Printed and bound in Great Britain by
Clays Ltd, St Ives plc

The HarperCollins website address is
www.harpercollins.co.uk

Contents

Acknowledgements

I would like to express my sincere thanks and gratitude to the following.

My mother Betty. I miss you.

My children Roberta and Dean, for their love and support.

My grandchildren Poppy, Freddie and Ava, for bringing so much happiness into my life.

Simon Trewin, my agent, and Claire Gill of Peters, Fraser & Dunlop, for their invaluable help in starting me on the road to writing this book.

Michael Doggart of publishers Harper Collins, for giving me the chance, and Tom Whiting, my editor, for all his advice and assistance.

And an especially big thank you to the wonderful Julie Welch, who not only helped me to tell my story, sharing many tears and much laughter along the way, and became a friend but who has also given me the confidence and encouragement to try my hand at a novel. I will always be grateful, Julie. Thank you.

Foreword

BY JIMMY TARBUCK

In the words of his adoring West Ham fans, Bobby Moore was a 'top geezer'.

The fact that he left us at fifty-one years of age is downright unfair. His memorial service was held at Westminster Abbey – how fitting for the best England captain we have ever had and for us all to say goodbye to our national hero. It was a wonderful service. Franz Beckenbauer read a lesson and then it was my turn. I have never been so nervous in my life. I opened up with, 'I usually say it's nice to be here, but on this particular day it certainly isn't.'

What I thought happened was that God had arranged a football match in heaven and had said to St Peter, 'Get me the best captain.' That, without doubt, was Bobby Moore.

He was a total gentleman and a very fair man, both on and off the pitch. He was a terrific companion who could have won the World Lager Drinking Championship three years running. He was totally let down by those small, envious men who controlled football on a national basis in those days. He was never once offered a job, a position as a football ambassador or just representing the England team. It was, and still is, a bloody disgrace. He deserved so much more from life. What a great Minister of Sport he would have made.

I once asked Pele about him. He said that Bobby wasn't a friend, he was a brother. After all these years I still can't believe that he's gone and the phone is not going to ring and that voice at the other end will say, 'Hello, Jimbo, all well?' His sense of humour and his companionship and him just being Bobby Moore – oh, I do miss him.

CHAPTER ONE

Hero

Here's my Bobby now. Head up, sunlight on blond curls. He's been out there for nearly two hours but he looks so elegant and calm he might just have stepped onto the pitch.

He's chesting the ball down. A short pass to Ballie, who passes it back, socks down around his ankles. Bobby looks up. Where to now?

I can feel Judith Hurst's fingers tighten on my arm. Out of the corner of my eye I catch sight of Geoff, exhausted but still instinctively heading for the German goal.

Oh Bobby, don't risk it. Big Jack Charlton's screaming at you. No one can hear what he's saying, all we can see is his Adam's apple wobbling, but it's what we're all thinking. *We're 3–2 up! We're in the final minute! Kick the %*#\$ thing into the stands!*

Judith and I are clinging to each other, the way we've done for most of the game. Every conceivable emotion has been wrung out of us – pride, rapture, excitement, despair, euphoria, disbelief, hope, agony, exhilaration. We clenched

1

our fists in anticipation when Martin Peters scored with twelve minutes to go. We plunged our heads in our hands when the Germans equalized with just moments of normal time remaining.

We watched the shot from Geoff bounce in off the crossbar in extra time. Or did it hit the underside and bounce out again? Wasn't it a goal after all? Judith was shouting, 'It's in, it's in!' and I was backing her up with, 'Oh yes, it's in!' The German supporters behind us were shouting back, 'No it isn't!' We must have sounded like the audience at a panto. But it was all right. Goal given. 3–2.

The World Cup is nearly ours.

Now the German supporters have fallen silent. A few seconds of tension seem like an eternity. Bobby finds Geoff, running way upfield, with the perfect ball. People start running onto the pitch. In living rooms all over the land Kenneth Wolstenholme is telling the nation, 'They think it's all over . . .'

Geoff's puffing out his cheeks, the way he always does when he shoots. The ball lands in the net. And to continue with those words of Kenneth Wolstenholme, which I think everyone in England must know by heart, '. . . It is now.'

There's too much noise to hear the final whistle, but around me is an explosion of delirious joy. I just sit in silence for a few seconds. I'm drained, physically and emotionally. The roller coaster of the last eighteen months that Bobby and I have lived through, the public adulation and success, the private terror and uncertainty, have suddenly got to me. I can't take this in.

I don't stay still for long, though. Judith and I are out of our seats, hugging each other. I think of Doss, Bobby's mother, who's spent every game of the tournament pottering around the garden because she can't bear the suspense of watching Bobby. Now she'll be so proud and overjoyed.

Bobby climbs the steps. He glances at the Queen's lily-white gloves and carefully wipes his sweaty, muddy palms on his shorts then dries them on the velvet balustrade before receiving the trophy. I can't help smiling. It's such an elaborately thoughtful gesture, so typical of Bobby. Mr Perfect.

And when he holds up the cup, I cry. Not out of happiness because England have won but because of what he's been through to be standing here today with the Jules Rimet Trophy in his hands. Watching him being carried round on his team-mates' shoulders, I just think how magnificent he is. Here's someone who, only a year and a half before, unknown to all but half a dozen people, has undergone a terrible ordeal with cancer and overcome it. Now he's every schoolboy's hero, holding up the World Cup. To me, that's the real magic of the day. What a man.

The thirtieth of July 1966 must be a date branded on every English person's memory for all time. Even people who weren't born then know about the day we won the World

Cup. It's part of British history. It was a unique occasion. Even if we won it again (wouldn't it be great?), the boys of summer 1966 will always have a special place in everyone's hearts. They were the first.

When I think back on that time, the sun always seems to be shining in my mind's eye, although in fact it rained on the afternoon of the Final. It must be something to do with the era in which it took place. The Boys of '66 were part of the fabric of the Sixties: Swinging London, the Harold Wilson government, student protests, flower power, the Beatles and the Stones, white boots and mini-skirts, Biba and Mary Quant. It was a gorgeous, glorious time when the whole of Britain seemed youthful, successful and optimistic.

As Judith Hurst and I were driven in an England bus with the rest of the wives past the throngs of people in Wembley Way that day, we felt so proud and full of expectation. And the first people we saw when we took our seats were Terence Stamp and Jean Shrimpton, who was probably *the* face of the Sixties. She looked so glamorous, absolutely stunning. I had done a little modelling for a couple of catalogues but I just wasn't in her orbit. She was the real thing. I couldn't take my eyes off her. She just stood out.

The build-up to the Final had been overwhelming. Wherever you went, it was all anyone talked about, but I could still hardly believe what was happening to us. Yes, it was a time when the class system was breaking down and people from ordinary backgrounds like us were beginning to become cultural icons. And yes, Bobby had already become football's first pin-up – Terry O'Neill's photo of him, surrounded by models, had appeared in an edition of *Vogue* in 1962. Not only that – he had just graced the fashion pages of the *Daily Express*, kicking a ball in a Hardy Amies suit. But this was something else again. Before the World Cup, I'd been able for the most part to go about with my family in anonymity. But in those weeks leading up to the Final I had my first taste of what it meant to be a celebrity, just for being married to a footballer.

I was being recognized in Bond Street. Shops would loan me designer clothes. Alfie Isaacs, a huge West Ham fan who owned an upmarket dress shop, gave me the outfit I wore on Final night – yellow silk chiffon with a flared skirt and a beaded top that I teamed with a tourmaline mink stole. Alfie had arranged for the photographers to be there when I tried it on and they followed me as I skipped up the road on a shopping spree. I caught sight of Alfie peering anxiously at me from round the corner, worrying that his ensemble was going to be upstaged.

Taxi drivers wouldn't charge fares. I discovered I could ring up a restaurant and say, 'Tina Moore here, can I have a table?' and the answer was never 'No'. Ford gave us a white Escort, although as it had World Cup Willie, a cartoon character, on the side, it wasn't the kind of vehicle you went anywhere in if you were trying to cultivate an impression of dignity. But let's be honest, we were having the time of our lives. Loads of doors opened for us because of Bobby's fame. I realized we were of value. A lot of it was hype and nonsense and I hadn't expected it, but it was great.

The point I'm making is that suddenly, for the first time ever, the game wasn't just something stuck at the back of the newspapers. Football had married fashion and now it was feature page material as well. In March that year, Terry O'Neill had taken some fabulous shots of Bobby and me, including one of me leaning against a tree in Epping Forest, wearing thigh-high boots and an England shirt as a mini-dress, while Bobby knelt at my feet wearing drainpipes and a black polo-neck. If we hadn't known it before, we knew it then – we were Bobby and Tina, the First Couple of football.

My picture also found its way into the *Sun*, where it formed part of a collection called 'Ten of the Best-Looking Women in England', probably because someone thought I looked a bit like Joyce Hopkirk; we both had long, blonde hair. There the similarity ended: she was the editor of *Cosmo* magazine and one of the most powerful, glamorous women in Fleet Street, while I was a Gants Hill housewife. And I hasten to say that it was a terrifically flattering photo of me – when I first saw it, I thought, 'Oh, she looks good' and carried on turning the pages. I hadn't recognized myself.

Don't get me wrong. I wasn't some new, unique star

in the firmament – Tina Moore, footballer's wife *extra-ordinaire*. It wasn't just me on whom the press were focussing. All the players' families found themselves to be of intense media interest. Martin Peters, Geoff Hurst and Bobby, the three West Ham players in the England side, all lived close by each other in suburban Essex and there were photoshoots in our back gardens, with toddlers crawling around our feet. Pictures of the girls of 1966 appeared in *The Sunday Times* – elegant Norma Charlton, pretty, coltish Lesley Ball, the lovely, warm Judith Hurst and tall, dark-haired Kathy Peters, looking haughty and *Vogue*-ish in her miniskirt. In actual fact, the real-life Kathy was one of the least haughty people you could ever meet. She had the most tremendous sense of fun. That girl was a real laugh.

I suppose, in a way, we were the prototype Footballers' Wives, but rather than being singers and models and celebrities in our own right, we were ordinary girls from ordinary backgrounds who only surfaced in the glare of publicity because we were married to the players. There was no pretentiousness or ostentation. Nobody was trying to cut anyone else out. There wasn't a big hairdo amongst us and we would have died rather than do anything that led to accusations of being flighty.

Really, we were girls of our time. We'd been brought up to respect our elders and betters and we certainly weren't swept away by our own importance. Set foot on the pitch or in the boardroom? We'd never have dared. At matches, the wives and girlfriends were always contained in a separate tea room, so if any of us harboured delusions of grandeur we soon got the message – we were of no consequence whatsoever!

For instance, on the evening of the World Cup Final there was a celebration dinner at the Royal Garden Hotel in Kensington High Street. Everyone was there: players and officials of the four semi-finalists, the World Cup organizing committee, the upper ranks of the Football Association. Everyone but the wives. The banquet was stag. In that era, not one of us found that at all remarkable and if Alf Ramsey said, 'No wives', then that was how it had to be. There was a wide gulf between managers and players in those days and not one of them would have questioned his decision. In our day we always did what we were told to do.

So we wives were herded into the Bulldog Chophouse in another part of the hotel. The only women allowed into the banquet were the official photographer, Sally Lombard, and her two assistants. One was Estelle Lombard, Sally's niece. The other was Betty Wilde – who just happened to be my mother.

The explanation? Sally Lombard's company, Jalmar, held the photographic concession at all the top London hotels. My mother was no photographer, but she and Sally were great, great friends. They went way back. As soon as it looked as if England would make the Final, the two of them hatched the idea between them. My mother kept it a tightly-guarded secret and Bobby and I were both astonished when she told us. What a coup! I wasn't jealous – far from it. I thought my mother was brilliant to have got herself in.

I didn't manage to set eyes on Bobby until around midnight, when photographers got us together for a picture on the roof terrace. Normally about as hot-headed as a snowman, that night he was a different man, wild with happiness and excitement, just radiating joy. The trophy was in his hands and I'm not sure who got kissed the more passionately, me or Jules Rimet.

As we left the hotel, I gasped – thousands of people were waiting outside just to get a glimpse of him. Bobby was so moved that he actually couldn't speak. As for me, that was the moment when it really sank in how much he meant to the fans. Forget the Prime Minister and Prince Charles, forget John Lennon, Paul McCartney and Mick Jagger. That night, Bobby was the most famous man in England.

It was a real shame that there wasn't a party laid on for the lads and the wives and girlfriends. It would have been lovely to celebrate together. Instead we all split up, with Bobby and I and a couple of the others heading for the Playboy Club. When we arrived everybody stood up and applauded. The atmosphere was just fizzing with electricity. Burt Bacharach was there with Victor Lownes, who ran the club and was Hugh Hefner's business partner, and he asked Victor to introduce him to Bobby. All the bunny girls were crowding round taking pictures. It ended up with Bobby on stage singing Stevie Wonder's 'One, two, three' – with hindsight, perhaps Geoff Hurst, the hat-trick hero, should have been up there singing that. And I had a song dedicated to me as well – 'My Cherie Amour'. What a fantastic night.

We got back to the hotel at around 3 am and tumbled into bed, dazed with happiness and triumph. The next day everyone went to the ATV studios, where the team appeared on a show hosted by Eamonn Andrews, and after that we went back to our house in Gants Hill on the eastern outskirts of London. It was our first marital home and cost £3,850. We'd started saving up for it the minute we got engaged at Christmas 1960.

Everyone came to terms with the events of the weekend in their different ways. Geoff Hurst mowed the lawn, then washed his car, the same as he did every Sunday afternoon. Martin and Kathy Peters had gone home early after the banquet because they had just bought a new house and Kathy had dealt with the move on her own while Martin was away with the England squad preparing for the World Cup.

Jack Charlton, several sheets to the wind, famously woke up in a sitting room in Leytonstone, having spent the night on the sofa of a complete stranger. When he tottered outside the next morning, a Geordie voice said, 'Hello, Jack!' from over the garden fence. It was a lady from his home town of Ashington, down in London for the weekend to visit relatives.

And the most celebrated man in England and his wife? With our heads still in the clouds, we held a party for our friends and re-lived the day. But after the guests had gone, everything just felt a bit flat, to be honest. Bobby poured himself a lager and tried to settle down to watch television, while I cleared up the glasses and looked back on the last eight weeks.

I'd loved every minute of it, of course I had. It had been heady and exhilarating, but a bit crazy, too. And with Bobby away with the team most of the time, I hadn't been able to share the fun with him. Now we were back to normality. It was time to come down off the clouds, I thought. I didn't know whether I felt relieved or bereft. Both, perhaps.

Whatever I thought normality was, we weren't back to it for long. I realized that when the telegram dropped onto the doormat a few days after the Final. It gave a date, followed by the message: PARTY STOP WOULD LOVE TO SEE YOU STOP LIONEL BART.

We were really excited and nervous. When we asked around, we found it was going to be a real showbiz party, so I went out to buy a new dress. It was green lace and knee-length. On the day I had my hair done specially, with a hairpiece that fixed on with an Alice band. Confident that

I truly looked the part, I set off with Bobby to Lionel Bart's house.

It was wonderful. I'd never been inside anything like it. The walls and ceiling of the guests' cloakroom were all mirrored and the loo itself was set in a huge golden chair. You really could claim to be 'on the throne'! Bobby and I were shown into a room full of guests. It was like walking into a photograph of a cross-section of Sixties glitterati.

Bobby and I weren't complete hicks. We were living in an age when working-class people were starting to make a lot of money in fashion and showbiz. Football was part of their roots, so naturally he was one of their heroes. We'd already started to rub shoulders with some of his up-and-coming East London contemporaries – Terence Stamp, who came from Plaistow, the same stamping ground as Martin Peters, was one of his drinking buddies, and Kenny Lynch, the entertainer, had been a mate ever since they'd met at the Ilford Palais, in the days when Bobby was captain of England Schoolboys.

Then there was Dougie Hayward, the so-called 'celebrity tailor' in Mount Street, Mayfair. Dougie, who made suits for Michael Caine, Tony Curtis, Peter Sellers, Kirk Douglas and the racing driver Jackie Stewart among others, was another East End boy who was mad about football. I bought Bobby one of his bespoke green velvet smoking jackets.

Johnny Haynes, the last England captain but one before

Bobby, had introduced us to the White Elephant, a private dining club in Curzon Street; it had been a favourite haunt of ours for a long time because Bobby was never interrupted by autograph-hunters there and we could enjoy a night out undisturbed. Because it attracted all the main stars of the time, we'd met Robert Mitchum, Sonny and Cher, and Sammy Davis Junior.

But this wasn't an exclusive club we were in; it was a celebrity's home. I quickly took in the presence of Tom Jones, Joan Collins, Anthony Newley, Alma Cogan, some of The Who, one of the Stones. The odd thing was that they were all sitting on the floor, though after a while I spotted an empty chair. By then, Bobby and I had had a couple of glasses of champagne for Dutch courage, so I clambered across all these famous people and sat down in it.

I had Joan Collins sitting on the floor on one side of me and Anthony Newley, her then husband, on the other.

'Who is she?' Joan Collins whispered to Anthony Newley as she looked up at me.

'I don't know,' said Anthony Newley, 'but I think she's sweet.'

The penny dropped. 'I'm not meant to be here,' I thought, and tripped back to where I'd come from. I had suddenly realized that the throne might have been in the loo but the chair was the next best thing, and the king who was meant to sit on it was Bobby.

Bobby was the son of a gas-fitter and I'd been a junior

secretary at Prudential Assurance. We'd always been in awe of these celebrities, but as far as they were concerned it was Bobby who was the star. As I looked around, watching them all queuing up to shake his hand, I studied what Joan Collins was wearing – a crocheted mini-dress and Courrèges boots, under one of those angled Mary Quant bobs.

'That's the last time anyone ever catches me in a knee-length dress and false hairpiece,' I thought. 'This is it. The big time. From now on, it's sink or swim.'

A few weeks later, I was faced with the choice of sinking or swimming again but this time literally. The government of Malta had invited Bobby and me to visit the island as representatives of the World Cup winning squad and we set off in great spirits, excited about seeing Malta and the neighbouring island of Gozo. Met by a tumultuous welcome, we felt close to achieving Royal status as we were taken on an open-topped motorcade tour of the local stadium.

That was where the problems started. Before the trip, inspired no doubt by my close proximity to Joan Collins, I'd had my blonde locks cut short at Vidal Sassoon. It was a disaster! I hated my new geometric hairstyle so much that I invested in a long blonde wig. It made me feel more like myself, but by the time we were roaring around Malta in the motorcade, it was shifting in the breeze and

I wasn't feeling very optimistic about its future prospects.

The wandering wig set the tone of a trip that had us alternating between shuffling exhaustion and convulsions of laughter. We had a very tight schedule and although the Maltese people were fantastically warm and hospitable, we were finding things very draining. Bobby only had to appear at the window of our hotel room in the mornings to be greeted with cheers and applause for, as he put it, 'the great feat of opening the curtains'.

So we were very grateful when they gave us one afternoon's rest, which allowed us to spend some time on a local businessman's yacht. The weather was gorgeous and we were offered the chance to water-ski. I had to refuse the invitation in case the blonde wig went walkabout, which was quite galling, although we did get to go on a speedboat and with the help of a red scarf I managed to keep my hair on. At the end of a fabulous afternoon, the speedboat bore us back to port where we were due to meet a prominent Maltese monsignor and a couple of government ministers.

It so happened that the day before our yacht visit, Bobby and I had run into Mike Winters, one half of the Mike and Bernie Winters comedy duo, and his wife, Cassie. They were holidaying out there. Cassie, who was heavily pregnant, turned out to be not just a lovely person but a real character. Not only that, but she must have been psychic as well. Her parting shot to me was, 'I've got a feeling about you. You're going to be front page news one day.'

In fact, her prophecy was proved right a little bit quicker than that. Within forty-eight hours the front page of *The Maltese Times* was carrying huge banner headlines saying: MONSIGNOR AND MRS BOBBY MOORE IN SEA DRAMA.

What happened was this. As our speedboat reached the shore, a gangplank was extended for us to climb off. Very gingerly I stepped onto it. At that moment there was a slight swell and I grabbed at the bishop's extended hand. It caught him off guard. Over my shoulder went one priest. As he went flying towards the water, the Minister of Sport tried to catch hold of him and fell in with him. With me already on the gangplank and Bobby about to step onto it, the boat rocked, the gangplank gave way and we went into the briny too.

It gets worse. The wig which I'd so carefully guarded all day was soaked and dyed red from the scarf. I must have looked like a victim of a shark attack, especially as my knees and shins were grazed and bleeding. I was wearing a navy crêpe mini-dress and that was up to a daring new high, so it was just as well the monsignor's glasses had fallen off and sunk to the bottom.

BOBBY MOORE IN HEROIC SEA RESCUE ATTEMPT? No way. He was far too busy desperately trying not to crack up with laughter, in case he hurt anyone's feelings. But the funniest thing was what my mother – ever my publicist – said when a reporter rang up for her reaction: 'Oh, I'm sure Tina's all right. She's a very strong swimmer.'

I was in the Cipriani restaurant recently, chatting with my friend Marilyn Cole, the British *Playboy* bunny who became Playmate of the Year, and we were talking about England's 2004 European Championship defeat by Portugal. I can't imagine that forty years ago a glamorous woman like Marilyn Cole would have been discussing whether a divot had caused David Beckham to miss a penalty.

It's different now. Can you imagine the World Cup winning captain of England going back to his Essex semi to sip lager and watch TV? Can you imagine the hat-trick hero being able to wash the car outside his house the next day without being mobbed?

There's no way today's up-and-coming football apprentice would have to bump up his pay by working as a labourer. Bobby did. In his teens he had a summer job at William Warnes, the factory where his mother worked. As it happens, that job and the chores he had to perform as a colt for West Ham – sweeping the stands and rolling the grass – were things he liked doing because they built him up; although he had strong thighs like tree trunks, his arms were like twigs. I think he knew he had the makings of an Adonis!

That Saturday in July 1966 changed everything. The

minute Bobby held up that trophy at Wembley, football was never going to be just a sport any more. It wasn't only the fact that England won, either. There was something about Bobby himself, his blond good looks, his style, the way he carried himself. You don't often hear a man described as beautiful, but that's what Bobby was. He looked like a young god – one who happened to play football.

He was a complicated young god. As a husband and father he was warm and loving. As a player he was cool and undemonstrative. His temper was so controlled and his tackling so accurate that he was almost never booked. He had a ruthless, calculating streak – if someone hurt him in a tackle, he would never react in the heat of the moment, but store it up for later and make his point when the time was right. To have that icy self-control turned against you was devastating, as one day I would discover. But those qualities were part of what made him the great England captain we all so admired.

Bobby and I were the first to experience the good and the bad of post-1966 football. We bought the dream house and lived the fabulous lifestyle. We were courted by Prime Ministers and befriended by celebrities. We had to cope with the glare of the media and the tensions which that caused in our marriage. We had kidnap threats to our children. All firsts.

Bobby's bonus for being part of the World Cup winning

side was £1,000. Now that seems like a pittance, but in any case to him that wasn't what it was about. It was about putting on that shirt with the three lions on the chest and hearing the roar of expectancy when he led the team out of the tunnel. Some kind of charge went through him the moment he put on that shirt. He seemed to turn into a lion himself.

I can see him now, the ball resting on his hip. Then he'd knock it into the air with the back of his hand before breaking into a jog, running with those little short steps and holding down the cuffs of his long-sleeved shirt with his fingers.

He was so proud of being an England player. He liked the fame, he loved the big crowd and above all he believed in his country. He showed it by the way he played. I think that's why he's remembered with such love and why so many people continue to look on him as the greatest English footballer there has ever been.

CHAPTER TWO

Wilde Women

If my mother and I hadn't been riding in a taxi along Ilford High Street that day in 1958, perhaps my life would have turned out very differently. Perhaps Bobby would have given up hanging around the local shops in the hope of catching sight of me. Perhaps he would have met another nice girl at the Ilford Palais and someone else entirely would have ended up with Judith Hurst clutching her arm at Wembley on 30 July 1966. Perhaps . . . But I'd better begin at the beginning.

My mother's name was Elizabeth Wilde, although everyone knew her as Betty. She was that rare combination – a woman who was beautiful *and* funny. We'd walk down the road together and men would whistle at her, not me. Even when she was in her late forties, they admired her. After Bobby and I were married, Bill Larkin, a wealthy West Ham fan, would regularly inform me that while I was a good-looking woman, 'You're not a patch on your mum yet.'

She definitely wasn't the average mother. For a start, she was a great cook – almost unique among post-war British housewives. But much more than that, she was one of those people you were drawn to in a crowded room. She had a zest for life and a strong sense of comedy and you wanted to bask in her warmth.

She was also incredibly wise and a tremendous listener. That's probably how, later on, she came to be a friend and a bit of a mother confessor to the West Ham lads. They'd go and talk to her for ages in the sports shop that in due course she ran for Bobby opposite the West Ham ground. Sometimes Bobby would invite her to join some of the players and go to the pub after training or a reserves game. They enjoyed her company and considered her to be one of them – she was an honorary lad. Quite a compliment, I felt. I was so proud of her.

I've always had the feeling that the moment she saw Bobby, she knew he would be right for me and decided she'd do everything she could to get us together. Life hadn't been all that easy for her. She'd always had to work for her living, because she and my father split up when I was two. After she died, one of her friends said to me, 'She was a film star. An absolute film star. She was absolutely stunning. And she had the most disastrous taste in men.'

Her friend got it exactly right. The three most important men in her life let her down badly in one way or another. I think that's why she was so keen to bring Bobby and me together. She was determined I wasn't going to make the mistakes she had made. It was my mother who saw how sweet and loving Bobby was to me and how much in love he was. I think she saw all the good qualities he had that perhaps I didn't discern at first. She could see that he was well-mannered, decent and courteous, as well as good-looking. She loved him and he loved her. When he and I started going out together, I sometimes teased her by saying that I thought she loved Bobby more than I did. I think he was a little bit in love with her, too.

I grew up in Ilford, a small, busy Essex town on the edge of East London. Ilford wasn't that far from Bobby's home town of Barking, but it was definitely regarded as a cut above socially, being quite middle-class and Tory. In those days its long High Street was looked on as a notable shopping Mecca and halfway along it was the boy-meets-girl factory, dance hall and theatre of Saturday night dreams, the Palais-de-Danse, where Bobby and I first set eyes on each other.

My first home was a semi in Christchurch Road. The house had two floors and my mother and I lived in the downstairs part. There was no need to separate the house into flats because it was all in the family – upstairs lived Aunt Molly, Uncle Jim and their three children, Jimmy, Marlene and Jenny. Jenny was three years younger than me and more like a little sister than a cousin. My mother's family were evacuated to Cornwall during the war but as my father had gone riding off into the sunset and my mother needed to be the breadwinner, Molly was summoned back from the West Country to be my childminder. It was a very female-dominated environment. After my father left, it was a long time before my mother had another serious relationship. She was the driving force in my life and I grew up without much experience of men's ways.

Our part of the house had a large living room at the front, with a smaller room behind it which served as my bedroom. If you went down a step and turned right, you'd find yourself in the scullery. You turned left for the cellar or went through to another large room with French doors that opened onto the garden. That was my mother's room. Once I started school I was a latchkey kid. If I couldn't reach it through the front door I'd have to climb in through the coalhole.

We had our own loo (outside), but the bathroom upstairs belonged to Aunt Molly and Uncle Jim. My mother and I went upstairs for a bath once a week and on the other days we made do with sitting in a tin bath for a good wash down – a chore because of all the heating up of kettles that had to take place. When it wasn't in use, the tin bath hung from a nail against the outside wall. Occasionally we couldn't face all the bother of getting it down and setting it up and took ourselves off instead to Ilford Baths. I can still remember those shouts of, 'More hot for Number Six!'

I don't want to leave the impression that I had a deprived childhood. It never felt like that at all. I was surrounded with love, tolerance and affection, so who cared if the place didn't boast 'all mod cons'? I remember my years in Christchurch Road as full of laughs and a lot of fun. I had good manners and politeness drummed into me gently but firmly, as well as the lesson that luxuries were there to be appreciated, not expected as a matter of course. I was a well brought up girl!

It wasn't as if it was anything out of the ordinary in those early post-war years. My friend Pat Booth, the author, photographer and former model whom I admire very much and who grew up a few streets away from Bobby, lived above a pie and mash shop. They had an outside loo, too, and a guard dog so scary that she would grab two pies whenever she went out there. One was to throw at the dog to distract it when she was leaving, and the other to throw at it so she could get back through the door unscathed on the return journey.

My mother was incredibly protective of me. One day, while I was taking a short cut through Valentine's Park on the way to school, a man flashed at me. I reported the incident to the park keeper, who promptly summoned the police. They asked me to tell them what happened, saying, 'Describe the man, not the implement.' When my mother arrived to collect me, she was as furious with me as if I'd committed an offence myself. 'It's boarding school for you,' she said. Of course, I got round her. I could twist her round my little finger. I realize now that she was frightened. I was 11 or 12 at the time and just starting to bloom. It must have been so difficult for her, having to keep me safe without my father around to share the responsibility.

Although money was tight, we were always very well dressed. This was thanks to a shop in Ilford High Road called Helene, which specialized in designer names. The great thing about Helene was that you could buy everything on something called 'the weekly', a kind of pay-as-you-wear scheme, and my mother never looked anything but smart and beautifully turned out.

I think some women felt jealous of her, in fact. For example, there was Mrs Marshall, who lived down our road with her two children, Vinnie and Bea. I used to go and play with them. Mrs Marshall was the kind of woman who would put butter on her own bread and give the children margarine, and she was teeth-grindingly envious of my mother's glamour. My mother had a hairpiece that was for special occasions – in that era it was called a switch. She would regularly wash it and peg it on the line to dry. One day when I was round at Vinnie's, he announced, 'My mum saw your mum's hair hanging on the line.'

'You liar,' I said, 'it was a yellow duster', and gave him a specially hard slap. I used to hit him quite a lot anyway, but that day he really got it. No way would he be spreading any more rumours about my mother, that was for sure.

When we became the only house in Christchurch Road with television, we were the talk of the street and the star attraction. The screen was eight inches wide and had a magnifying glass strapped to it. The Marshalls and all the other children in the road used to stand on the window sill to look at it and when the show was ready to begin, Jenny and I would part the lace curtains.

In fact, it was a wonder that we didn't charge them. That was what we did with the kids who came to watch the shows Jenny and I put on in the back garden. I was the ringmaster and Jenny the very bossed-about entertainer. When she became fed up of jumping through hoops, the family dog would be dressed up and brought in as her understudy. Meanwhile, Jenny would be made to hang by her knees from the laburnum tree – the highlight of the show. I was in charge of magic tricks.

Jenny and I used to ride on the horse-drawn milkman's float, too. We sat up top with the milkman, so it was a great treat to be selected to help. When the rag-and-bone man was on his rounds, we would ask all the neighbours to give us their old clothes because that would qualify us for a goldfish each. The two of us also used to sneak out and have midnight feasts with the other children in the street. You just couldn't do that sort of thing now. It was a fantastic childhood, despite the lack of money.

Jenny's mother, Aunt Molly, was known to me as Auntie

Mum. I can't have been the easiest child to look after. Probably because my mother felt so guilty about going out to work and leaving me, she wouldn't allow Auntie Mum to discipline me and I used to do naughty things like throw the other children's toys downstairs. I was just like the girl in the nursery rhyme: 'When she was good she was very, very good, and when she was bad she was horrid.'

In my defence, all I can say is that I missed my mother. Auntie Mum was sweet, soft, kind and easy-going and I adored her, but all the same I was acutely aware that my three cousins had their mother around all day to look after them and I didn't have mine. The highlight of my day was waiting for her to come home.

I was so possessive about her that I didn't like her boyfriend Joe at all. He was quite rich and must have had a few contacts in the black market – not only was he a reliable source of silk stockings but we were treated to a constant supply of eggs, butter and sugar, all luxuries at the time. Something else we never went short of was smoked salmon. I even had it in the sandwiches I took to school. In the end I got so bored with smoked salmon sandwiches that I'd go round swapping them for ones made with jam.

In many ways she had a sad time, my mother. I think Joe was really the love of her life, but although he claimed to be separated from his wife, he never committed. She was a real beauty and a lively, bright, talented woman, but she got a lot less than she deserved. She was a blonde and looked like Virginia Mayo, a Hollywood star of the Forties and Fifties. She wore her hair drawn back into a French pleat, which showed off her classic features, and she always had an air of elegance. My grandmother, Nanny Wilde, used to say she was the flower of the flock – and it was a pretty big flock. My mother was one of seven children, five of whom were girls. She wasn't short of brains and when she was 11 she won a scholarship to high school, but she wasn't allowed to take it up. My grandmother said it wouldn't be fair on her sisters.

It was Uncle Jim, my mother's brother, who was Nanny Wilde's favourite. He and my Aunt Glad held the European professional title for ballroom dancing. That was quite something. Jim owned a dance hall, the Princes, in Barking; coincidentally, it wasn't far from Waverley Gardens, where Bobby grew up. Nanny Wilde ran the café at the back.

In those days, the Forties and early Fifties, ballroom dancing was huge. No one had TV then, of course, so everyone made their own entertainment by going out to dances and music halls. There was no such thing as a couch potato then. When my mother was in her teens, she was a very good dancer. People reckoned she had the ability to be even better than Jim and she was selected to appear in a talent show. She would have earned 2s. 6d. a week – not a sum to be sneered at sixty years ago – but Nanny Wilde put a stop to that, too.

Why? I can only speculate. My grandmother was an

old-fashioned matriarch, a bit of a tyrant. She was a very powerful woman who ruled with an iron fist, and she was tough. She probably had to be, with seven children. She was such a strong personality that she seemed almost to obliterate my grandfather. Pop Wilde had a bowler hat and a walking stick and that's just about all I remember of him.

The Wilde household lived 'round the corner', to use East London parlance. In actual fact they were a bit further away than that, in a large detached house in Cranbrook Road, Gants Hill. It had a monkey puzzle tree in the front garden and a marvellous lilac tree in the back. But everyone you knew used to live 'round the corner' if they didn't live 'over the road'.

There wasn't only Nanny, Pop and the kids. Archie, the lodger, was part of the equation as well. It was rumoured that the two youngest of the Wildes – my mother and her sister, Eileen – were Archie's, not Pop's. It's certainly true that Eileen didn't look anything like Pop and if the rumours are to be believed, that might explain why Nanny was tough on my mother – she might have reminded her of her indiscretion.

I've got to say that Nanny Wilde was never tough on me – it was only my mother with whom she had the difficult relationship. I'd go round there frequently and listen as she played the piano and sang. She was very family-orientated and I adored her. It was being so family-orientated that got Nanny Wilde into trouble one night at the dance hall, a night so dreadful that for years we could hardly bear to speak of it.

The biggest dance event of the year, the Star Championships, was held up in London and Uncle Jim and Aunt Glad were favourites to win it. The whole family dressed up to the nines to go and watch. My mother even went to the furriers and borrowed two coats on approval for her and Nanny Wilde. It was all heady and exciting stuff and by the time Jim and Glad finished doing their routine, Nanny Wilde had had a few drinks. She swept up to one of the woman judges, pointed to her earrings and told her that she would look better in a different pair.

Unfortunately, the judge had a sense of humour failure, construed the earrings remark as attempted bribery and marched off to report Nanny Wilde to the powers that be. Shortly afterwards, it was announced over the tannoy that Glad and Jim had been disqualified. Oh, the shame of it. And the fur coats had to go back the next day. It was a nightmare!

I think what really drove a wedge between my mother and Nanny Wilde was that she, Betty, was a modern girl – ahead of her time, a bit wilful, perhaps. By the time she was 17 she was virtually living away from home, staying with the family of Gladys Mogford, her best friend. The Mogfords loved her, almost as if she was their own. And I think that in the end she decided to get married, even though she was very young, rather than go home. She just got out.

I know she loved my father, but getting married was really an escape route from her unhappiness. The only trouble was, what she escaped into turned out to be no better than what she'd left behind. My father left her for another blonde when I was very little. After that there was Joe, with his half-truths and broken promises. When I was 12, she got married again, to a ship's chef called Eddie, but that didn't work out either.

She'd had so many disappointments and frustrated ambitions that she projected her dreams onto me. She definitely believed I was destined for greater things. I was groomed and always beautifully turned out. Because she didn't want me to be a gorblimey Cockney, I was sent to elocution lessons. I've no idea why my mother thought it was a good idea, but for some reason I was also packed off to fencing lessons.

At one point I joined a dancing school, where they were about to stage a show including 'The Good Ship Lollipop'. I was hastily given a part in it, although as I was a new-comer, the role was minuscule. Not that you would have known. Every mother was given her child's costume to tart up and mine had at least ten times more ribbons and bows than the star's did. In fact, compared to me, Shirley Temple herself would have found her outfit wanting.

It all went to my head. At the end of the performance, when we all lined up to take a bow, someone with a bouquet stepped onto the stage. I might have been stuck right at the end of the line, but I knew what I was worth! I skipped forward and said, 'Thank you.' They had to wrest the bouquet off me. I was in floods of tears. So that was the end of my theatrical career.

Much to my mother's surprise, I passed the 11-plus and was offered a place at Ilford County High School, which had the reputation of being both strict and highly academic. My mother was actually so worried when she received the letter containing the Ilford High offer that she asked the Head of my primary school if she should turn it down. She really had doubts about my coping. I was bright enough, just not terribly keen on schoolwork.

The Head assured her I'd be fine there and, as it turned out, I was. I didn't like school very much, though, particularly grammar school. It was an alien world of Latin, French and German, indoor sandals, dresses that couldn't be more than an inch off the floor when you knelt down, and heel grips. Heel grips were as much part of the Fifties as paper nylon petticoats and headscarves worn over hair rollers on Friday nights, and your mum made you stick them in your outdoor shoes which had been bought for you to grow into.

I wasn't a total failure. I was picked for the hockey team, showed willing by joining the fencing club and had a very nice English teacher called Miss Mackie, who didn't seem much older than her pupils. Years later our daughter, Roberta, then 10, won a place at the City of London School for Girls. Bobby and I travelled up to the Barbican with her for her interview and when we were admitted into the Headmistress's study, there was Miss Mackie! I seemed to grow younger and smaller by the second as I turned into Tina Dean from Christchurch Road with her heel grips and failure to appreciate the finer points of Shakespearean plays.

'I can only hope Roberta does better than me,' I faltered.

Miss Mackie looked at Bobby, then nudged me. 'Oh, I think you did *very* well, dear,' she said, with a bit of a wink.

Once it was confirmed that I didn't have a glittering academic future, my mother decided to get me onto the books of a modelling agency. We went to their head-quarters so they could take a look at me and we were waiting to be seen when we overheard the receptionist answering the phone. As she was taking down all the details out loud, we realized that the caller was trying to book one of the agency's models.

'Quick,' hissed my mother and dragged me out into the street, where she hailed a cab and hustled me into it. The next moment, she was telling the cabbie to take us to the address we'd just heard trip off the lips of the receptionist.

When we got there, my mother announced to the client that I was the model sent by the agency. Looking a bit dubious (I was only 15), the client gave me a coat to try on. I did my best, but he received the coat back from me impassively and invited my mother to try it on. As soon as he saw her in it, he offered her the job! I think that was when my mother realized that I wasn't going to be a star myself, so I'd better aim for the next best thing, which was to marry one.

By that time my mother had been married to Eddie, the ship's chef, for three years. I was 11 when she first introduced him to me and at the time I liked him. I was still quite innocent and impressionable and it never crossed my mind that he was playing up to me in the hope that I'd accept him, unlike all my mother's other suitors, which would earn him Brownie points with my mother. I think the fact that I tolerated him where I'd rejected the others probably clinched it for Eddie where my mother was concerned.

When she told me she was getting married, I was so pleased that I immediately started imagining what I'd wear and how I would look with my hair permed in a style called 'Italian Boy'. But the evening before her wedding, I went to show her my dress, which was white with a floral print and made of paper nylon, and found her crying on the phone to her friend, Sally Lombard.

Although I'll never know for certain, I'm convinced that

she realized she was making a mistake, that she'd only agreed to marry Eddie because she was weary of Joe's broken promises and because life as a single parent was tough and she longed for a bit of security and support. But Joe was the man she really loved and in any case, Eddie wasn't as nice as we thought. It was only when he was wooing my mother that he tried to win me over by being as sweet as pie to me. After the wedding, we started to see the other side of him – from sweet as pie to sour as lemons. In the end he took himself off back to sea and that was the last we heard of the Dreaded Eddie.

So when my mother met Bobby, I think she thought, 'Here's a decent man.' She met his parents, Doris and Bob, who had been married for ever. She saw the stable background he'd come from and she wanted that for me. She didn't want me to re-live her life.

CHAPTER THREE

When Bobby Met Tina

My mother and I used to walk past Ilford Palais on the way to the Regal cinema and I'd look yearningly at it and think I'd never be old enough or glamorous enough to go there.

On the ceiling was a glittering, twinkling ball of mirrored mosaic, spinning and throwing off lights. The girls would put their handbags on the floor and dance round them. The cha-cha was the fashionable dance and there would be a long trail of boys and girls doing it in sync, like line-dancing. I used to think it was so adult and I longed to be part of it.

There was a Babycham bar. Babycham was the drink *du jour*; it was sparkly and bubbly like champagne, although actually it was made from pears. It came in tiny bottles with a Bambi on the label blowing bubbles from its mouth. You drank it from a proper champagne glass, feeling like sophistication come to life.

The Palais was packed with young people. It featured live bands like Ambrose and his Orchestra. A man called

Gerry Dorsey sang with the band, but failed to achieve any great fame until he recorded a song called 'Please Release Me' and simultaneously had the inspired idea of changing his name to Engelbert Humperdinck.

Another of Ambrose's singers was Kathy Kirby. She looked like Marilyn Monroe, with fabulous platinum blonde hair and glossy red lipstick and a soaring soprano voice. In the early Sixties she went on to have a huge hit called 'Secret Love', but in those Ilford days she and her sister, Pat, lived virtually opposite us. I'd see her in the window of her front room, wearing a satin cat suit and walking around holding the phone on a very long wire, which to me was the height of chic. Pat was quite something, too. She married Terry Clemence, who owned the Seven Kings Motor Company, and they had three daughters who all went on to make brilliant marriages, one to a viscount, the other two to lords. Not bad going for three car dealer's girls from Essex.

I wasn't to know then, but Pat and Terry would one day become near neighbours of Bobby and me in Chigwell. We lived it up at many a party. But that was all years into the future . . .

The big day came when I finally made it to the Palais. I'd been off school with flu since the start of the week and my mother had been trying to build up my strength with nourishing invalid breakfasts of bread in warm milk with sugar before she headed off for work. Towards the end of the week I started feeling better and concocted a plan with a school friend, Vivien Day, to go to the Palais for the lunchtime session. This started at twelve and as my mother didn't get back from work until early evening, I knew I could get back home and into my sickbed without her being any the wiser.

That morning she treated me to the bread-and-milk as usual. Yuk. Who wants that when you're heading for the Babycham bar? She was really worried because I only picked at it, and to tempt back my appetite left me Irish stew, my favourite, for my lunch.

The stew went untouched. Instead, Vivien and I were tremblingly shelling out 6d. each at the door of the Palais. Sixpence was the lunchtime cheap rate. In new money, it translates into the staggering sum of 2½p.

My heart was beating like a hammer as I advanced into the place that I'd dreamed of for so long. I just looked and looked. It was crowded with people of my own age, most of whom had nipped out during school lunch hour. I was particularly awestruck by the ladies' cloakroom. The walls were panelled in rich, plum-coloured velvet. The fittings were gilt. It was lit by chandeliers. I was amazed.

When I got home, still starry-eyed, my mother was waiting for me. I'd forgotten that Thursday was her half-day. The lamb stew was thrown straight into the dustbin. As far as she was concerned, it was the most heinous thing I'd done since getting myself flashed at in Valentine's Park. It was boarding school for me again, for all of twenty-four hours.

The Ilford Palais episode wasn't my only covert expedition. I used to sneak up to the Two I's with my girlfriends to see Tommy Steele, but things would hardly have started before we had to steal away at 10 pm like Cinderella. Another place we went to was Heaven and Hell, which was in a basement accessed only by some very narrow stairs. If a fire had broken out, it would have been virtually impossible to escape. But you never think of that kind of thing when you're 15. You're immortal.

My first boyfriend was Harry and I went out with him for six months. He was 17 and had lovely amber-coloured eyes with long eyelashes. Harry was a Mod and wore a bum-freezer jacket; he took me to haunts like the Skiffle Parlour in Ilford Lane on the back of his scooter. But that Easter I was offered a school trip to Perpignan, and my mother said, 'I think it would be a good idea if you went on that.' She had no time for Harry, amber eyes or not.

No sooner had she removed me from the clutches of Harry than I fell for Gilbert, the Perpignan Adonis. He played rugby for France schoolboys and was my first real crush. Cupid's dart must have been more of a pinprick, though, because Gilbert was soon abandoned in favour of my next conquest, an actor. He can't have been a very successful one because I've forgotten his name. But he had some great lines. 'When you grow up,' he murmured, 'you're going to be quite something. You must always drink champagne with a peach at the bottom of the glass.'

My suitors also included the one who arrived to pick me up in a Jag. The Jag was nearly as old as he was. When he knocked on the door, my mother opened it and said, 'Can I help you?'

'I've come to see Tina.'

My mother said, 'Do you know how old she is? Fifteen.'

'Well, I like them young.' Off he went, never to be sighted again.

And then came Bobby.

'Blue Moon, you saw me standing alone
  Without a dream in my heart
  Without a love of my own.'

It's true. It really happened that way. The band at the Ilford Palais was playing 'Blue Moon' and suddenly this blond boy was in front of me, asking for a dance. Bobby always had an incredible knack of staging things to perfection.

To him, I suppose, I was a pretty girl in a lovely dress. Pat Booth, who went to the Palais at around the same time as me, said she'd catch sight of me in a boat-necked long-sleeved number and feel deeply envious – which was funny, because I used to lust after her clothes, a 'mod' dress, bell-skirted, with cap sleeves. I discovered later that

40

she also went out at one point with Harry the Mod; it must have been those amber eyes. After that she went out with one Billy Walker, who was a bouncer at the Palais, though not for much longer. He was just passing through on his way to becoming the golden boy of British heavyweight boxing

Bobby would go to the Palais with some of his fellow apprentices from the West Ham ground staff. Much later I found out that he'd been watching me for weeks, stationed on the balcony but too shy to approach me. What did Bobby see in me? I spoke nicely, I'd led a sheltered life and my mother had groomed me to the best of her ability. All those elocution lessons, dancing lessons and my grammar school education had combined to turn me into what, in the late Fifties, was called 'a nice type of girl'. I'm not sure that the fencing lessons ever came in useful, but my sense of humour did. I could make him laugh and this intense, rather inhibited football prodigy needed that.

Once you're in a relationship, you get to know and trust the other person and then your real self starts to unfold. Bobby unfolded a lot. Even now, I have a very strong image of him as a teenager, just sitting watching me, laughing because I amused him. I was the extrovert of the partnership and that's what he enjoyed about me. I brought him out of his shell. I could always twist things to see the funny side and although Bobby projected a public image of self-control and aloofness, he actually had a very dry wit.

41

It was so subtle that unless you were completely attuned to him, you missed it.

When we met, I was coming up to my sixteenth birthday. He seemed a bit square at first. Because I'd grown up in such a female-dominated environment, I knew nothing about football. I wasn't at all impressed that Bobby was a player, let alone that he had just signed professional forms with West Ham and was an England Youth international. I didn't even realize he *was* a footballer at first, not a proper one who was planning to make a career out of the game.

His great heroes were Johnny Haynes, captain of England, and the Manchester United icon, Duncan Edwards, with whom he was besotted. I hadn't a clue who he was talking about – didn't even realize that Duncan Edwards, one of the Busby Babes, had died along with seven of his team-mates earlier that year in the Munich air crash. Duncan had been a left-half and was already established in the England side, despite his tender age. Bobby was shattered when he heard the news.

He was much more taken with me than I was with him in the early stages. After that first dance I agreed to meet him at the Palais the following Saturday – then I stood him up. He waited all evening for me.

I'd told him I liked going to the record store, so he took to lurking around there in the hope that I'd walk in, but the most he would get from me was a little nod of acknowledgement. Even so, something about him must have made an impression because I told my mother about him. That was when Fate took a hand. One day, my mother and I were sitting in the back of a taxi as it crawled along Ilford High Street in the traffic when I happened to glance out of the window. There he was, sitting in a coffee bar. 'That's him!' I exclaimed. 'That's the boy who asked me out.'

My mother leaned across me to get a better view. 'Mm, he looks nice,' she said. 'Why don't you invite him home for tea?'

Our first date took place the evening after his second game for the West Ham first team. Bobby had made his first team debut at Upton Park when West Ham, newly promoted to the top flight, had beaten Manchester United 3–2. Bobby, only brought into the side because senior players were unfit, had been brilliant. He dominated the following day's back page headlines.

It was actually a bitter-sweet moment for Bobby when he got his first team chance, because his rival for the Number Six shirt was Malcolm Allison, who had been Bobby's mentor and idol since Bobby joined the club as a schoolboy. For most of 1958, they had both been fighting to get out of the reserves, Bobby because he was knocking on the door to his future, Malcolm because he was trying to prove he could still play after a spell in a sanatorium recovering from TB.

Malcolm was thirteen and a half years older than Bobby. Very tall, big-shouldered and handsome, he was a man, whereas Bobby was a boy. He had a slightly sardonic air and sometimes he could be cutting. It would be a while before he developed his twin reputations as fedora-wearing, cigar-smoking playboy and brilliant, flamboyant, big-spending coach, but even then he had panache. More than that, he could tell greatness in the raw. As one of thirteen colts on the ground staff at Upton Park, Bobby had been widely regarded as ordinary, but Malcolm saw something in him that others at the club didn't and set about coaching him. For that alone, Bobby adored him.

So Bobby's first-team debut brought mixed feelings. He was thrilled, but sorry it had happened because of Malcolm's illness. Malcolm, for his part, didn't bear a grudge. Bobby was his favourite son. Who better to replace him?

Five days after Bobby's dream debut, the complete opposite happened against Nottingham Forest. He had a terrible game, with the huge crowd shouting to the Forest players, 'Play on the left-half, that's the weak link.' West Ham lost 4–0. Bobby bought an evening paper at Nottingham station and the report on his performance was so damning that he tore it up. He hadn't any inkling that the last thing I'd be interested in was the football results.

Anyway, I had my own cross to bear. Having spent all afternoon preparing for our date and having my hair specially set for the occasion, I went to meet him at King's Cross. In those days it was a sooty Victorian edifice with iron gates controlling access to the platforms and huge steam engines fuelled by coal. When I heard the familiar grinding of the wheels and saw Bobby's train chugging to a stop, I decided to position myself where the steam gently wafted from the engine. I had visions of the mist slowly lifting and me emerging like the mysterious heroine of a romantic movie into a bedazzled Bobby's path. Sadly, that was not to be. The steam had other ideas and I came out looking like orphan Annie, with the hair that had been so carefully coiffed hanging limp and damp round my forlorn face.

I did think Bobby was great-looking, of course. He didn't have spots – well, occasionally a couple, but only very, *very* small ones. He was a terrific dancer; whatever he did, he had to be Mr Perfect. We used to kiss in time to the music. It was heady stuff! Looking back, though, it was so innocent.

The reason I found him a bit square was probably that he'd led a very disciplined life compared to most boys in the Fifties. He and the amber-eyed Harry were around the same age, but Bobby seemed not much more than a baby, really.

Doris was the dominant figure in the Moore marriage and in Bobby's childhood, and she was fiercely protective of him. She called him 'My Robert'. She was a very strong character and I think she recognized a similar strength in me. It was a while before we had a relaxed, easy relationship. In contrast, I got on immediately with Bobby's dad, Big Bob. He was a gas-fitter and came from Poplar. He was much more Cockney than Doris, was prematurely bald and liked clowning around and wearing silly hats. His childhood had been tough – he lost his father in World War One – but he was a lovely, kind man with a wonderful twinkle in his eye. He was straight-talking with it, though. He would tell you if he thought you were wrong.

In some ways Doris, who was always known as Doss, was a bit of a rebel by her family's standards. Most of them were Salvation Army. They used to go out on a Sunday carrying the Good Book, singing the hymns and wearing the bonnets – the whole ten yards, in fact. Maybe Doss started off by going with them but decided it wasn't for her – she was an independent-minded individual. Even so, she and Big Bob were very upright, God-fearing people.

Their terraced house in Waverley Gardens had a front fence where Big Bob always chained his bike. The first time I stayed round there, I was put in the box room. Doss cornered me there. 'Any girl,' she said, 'who gets My Robert into trouble will have me to deal with.'

My mother was absolutely furious when I told her. Floored, livid and silent with rage. But she soon recovered her powers of speech. 'You weren't brought up to be a floozy!' she gasped.

She was right. I was an innocent. Bobby and I did our courting in the pre-pill era. A girl I had been to school with died after a back-street abortion. I read about it in the local paper and felt horrified and frightened. But Doss's words hung over me. I never got Her Robert into trouble.

Neither Doss nor Big Bob smoked or drank alcohol and Bobby realized that my mother was much more worldly and sophisticated than them. When the time came for him to introduce them to the mother of the girl he loved, he bought gin and wine for them to serve. Meanwhile, my mother had realized that Doss and Bob Moore were teetotallers. Wanting to make a good impression, she said, 'I'd love a cup of tea' when Doss asked her what she would have.

Equally beside herself to impress, Doss came back with, 'Cow's milk, sterilized or condensed?' It became a running joke between Bobby and me whenever anyone asked what we'd like to drink.

Actually, Doss could never accept that Bobby could put away a lager or four. If he'd had too many, she'd say he was 'under the weather'. Quite a few years later, one Christmas after Bobby and I were married, he and a lot of the other West Ham lads went out at lunchtime to celebrate the festive season. Christmas Eve always seemed to be a bit of a nightmare for me. There'd been a couple of times earlier when the turkey, West Ham's annual

Christmas present, would go walkabout instead of coming home. Each time it would be spotted sitting on the bar, with Bobby ordering a lager for himself 'and a gin and tonic for the bird'. They'd eventually find their way home with the turkey propped up in the front seat.

On this particular occasion, Bobby and I were due to go to a function in the West End that night but by mid-afternoon, when he and the turkey still hadn't made it home, I began ringing round all his known haunts. Eventually I tracked him down to the Globe in Stepney and reminded him about the function.

'I'll be home in twenty minutes,' he said.

I waited for an hour, then rang again. 'Don't worry,' said my increasingly merry husband, 'I'll finish my drink and be on my way.'

So I waited another hour, then rang again. 'If you don't come home right now, I'll tell your parents to come and get you,' I said.

Even that didn't flush him out, so I carried out my threat. Doss and Big Bob duly set out for the Globe, where they advanced on him from the rear. Doss laid a hand on his shoulder and said, 'Home, son.'

'Mum,' said Bobby as they escorted him out, 'I'm 31.'

Doss turned and said to the assembled company, 'He isn't usually like this, you know. He's been under the weather lately.'

*   *   *

Bobby was their only child, and Doss and Big Bob adored him. He was Mr Perfect, their reason for being. The only bad thing he'd ever done was pee in a milk bottle – disgusting! Doss was involved in everything Bobby did, from supporting him at every single match he played in to washing, bleaching and scrubbing his laces with a nailbrush to make sure they stayed sparkling white, then ironing them.

It was Big Bob and Doss who took me to Upton Park for my first visit. I'd never been to a match before and I couldn't believe the number of people there. We sat in D Block with all the other players' families, behind the Directors Box, and Doss barely took her eyes off Bobby the whole game. She kept shouting, 'Unload him! Unload him!' I thought it was a technical term.

Doss had been very pretty as a girl; she'd won a beauty contest and you could see who Bobby got his looks from. Our daughter, Roberta, has inherited her lovely nose. And she was a very good woman: unaffected, modest, generous to those she loved, and natural. But she was a Scorpio and a typical one in some ways. She would harbour grudges. If anyone said anything bad about Her Robert, that would be it for them. They'd be completely cut out, for good and all time.

It wasn't just her looks that were handed down to Bobby. A lot of his personality traits, like his repressed, uptight side, came from her, too. They were both strict with themselves, both terribly disciplined, almost obsessively immaculate. Even after a late, lager-fuelled night, Bobby would get a clothes brush out and brush his whole suit down before turning in. Everything he did had to be faultless, and that was his mother's way too.

She used to cut and edge little 'Vs' in the side of his shorts just the way he liked them, so naturally when I leapt onto the scene I decided that that was going to be my job from then on. The first time I did it, they split all the way up to the waist during a match, so the first time was also the last. Doss got her job back. My Vs just didn't cut the mustard.

I also discovered she was a wonderful knitter, so I embarked on making Bobby a hideous green V-neck sweater. I did aspire, but she set such a terribly high standard. Whenever I ate round at Waverley Gardens, she would serve the mashed potato in exact half-moon shapes, using an ice cream scoop. The cuffs and collars of Bobby's shirts were always as smooth as glass. She'd never rush anything as crucial as the ironing. But as I've said, she and Big Bob were good people, and Doss was a little wounded and put out when Bobby fell in love with me. She felt he'd excluded her from his life. But again, that was Bobby – he only ever had one passion at a time. He met me and that was it. He was absolutely besotted.

Bobby also realized that his mum was possessive and he rebelled against that to a certain degree. It wasn't that he cut any ties with his parents. Once we were married, we constantly went round on visits. He was never derogatory about them. It was just that the intimacy, the sense of having one single, special person you shared your world with, had been transferred to me. He shut off from Doss emotionally. It must have hurt.

Bobby might have been young and a bit square, but he was very romantic and he had exquisite taste. He would send me flowers and place little *billets doux* under my pillow or in the pocket of my coat. He also had good design and technical skills; if the football hadn't worked out for him, he'd planned to train as a draughtsman. Once, when I was away for a few days, he redecorated my bedroom as a surprise. He turned a little filing cabinet into a jewellery box and re-upholstered the tub chair in red satin with black buttons. It probably sounds horrendous, but it looked gorgeous.

He was also very generous. I would receive complete outfits as a surprise. Once, after I had admired what my friend Anita Barker was wearing, he phoned her to ask her to get something similar for me. He even bought a dress off her back once. By the time he went with England to play France, his taste was developing nicely. I received a pink suit, navy blue blouse with pussy-cat bow and a Paco Rabanne chain mail bag.

When I was 17, we went on holiday to Italy – separate

bedrooms, of course – where he presented me with a skirt and paper nylon petticoat he'd just bought. For all his macho credentials as a footballer, in some ways he was one of the most untypical men I would ever meet. Later on, after we were married, he used to help me do my hair and I'd sit there thinking, 'If only the fans could see him now. The captain of England is bleaching my roots.' He loved going shopping and – even more bizarre – he actually liked shopping for clothes with me. That isn't a job for the faint-hearted.

I'd left school by then to start my job as a junior secretary at the Prudential Assurance Company in Holborn. Every evening when Bobby wasn't playing, he'd come up to meet me. I saw him every night bar Fridays, when he had to prepare for the match the next day. That was the night I could catch up on my girlie things and drive my mother mad because I'd monopolize the phone, talking to him for hours. He was shy and unsure of himself but he was determined to succeed in football and determined to have me. He already had nicknames for me – he called me Pet or Teen or, later, Percy, which was usually shortened to Perce. But I liked it best when he called me My Princess, and he certainly treated me as one.

One of our haunts was Sheekey's fish restaurant in the West End, which I introduced him to. It was my mother's favourite and I'd often gone there with her; we'd eat steamed Dover sole with lobster sauce and gaze at the

Beverly Sisters, who were regulars there. Joy, Teddy and Babs were then at the peak of their fame as the British answer to America's Andrews Sisters. Joy, a tall, lovely, slightly toothy blonde, went on to marry Billy Wright, England football captain of the Fifties. They were the Posh 'n' Becks of *their* day!

For Bobby and me, going to the Spaghetti House in Soho was a big deal, too. Neither of us had ever tried spaghetti before. It was fun trying to master the art of twirling the fork, although of course Mister Get-it-right-or-forget-it watched and observed how it was done before attempting a mouthful. We had a bottle of chianti in a straw basket and thought how sophisticated we were.

That night, on the way back through the West End, we found a shop selling little glass animals. It was still open and Bobby went inside and bought one for me. 'I love you,' he said. For the first time.

In a romantic daze, we missed the last bus from the station. I thought he'd be irritated, having to walk me home then get himself back to Waverley Gardens.

'Doesn't matter,' he said at the front door of Christchurch Road. 'I'll turn it into a training jog.'

'What, to burn off the spaghetti?'

'Yeah. Anyhow, I'm so happy I don't care about missing the bus. Goodnight, Princess.'

Silly, but sweet and true.

CHAPTER FOUR

And Big Mal Came Too

Our romance progressed more smoothly than Bobby's football career at first. As a result of the disastrous game at Nottingham in September 1958 he was dropped by West Ham's manager of the time, Ted Fenton, and didn't become a first team regular until the 1960–61 season after the first-choice defender, John Smith, was sold to Spurs.

Boosted by Bobby's new-found career stability, we got engaged on Christmas Day, 1960. Bobby was 19 and I was 17. Naturally, the proposal was planned and carried out in style. He'd even asked my mother's permission beforehand. That meant she knew what was in that big parcel, with my name on it and tied up with a huge bow, that I had been prodding expectantly ever since it had appeared a few days earlier under the Christmas tree in Christchurch Road.

We were due to go that night to a party at Nanny Wilde's, as we always did at Christmas, but I had a terrible cold and wasn't really looking forward to it for once.

'My nose is red,' I complained to Bobby, 'and besides, I haven't got anything to wear.'

Bobby grinned, then picked up the parcel and placed it in my arms. When I opened it, I found a brown and black check mohair skirt and a mohair jumper.

'I want you to wear those,' Bobby said, 'when you put on what's inside that.' He pointed to another box, a very small one, nestled in the folds of the outfit. I opened up the small box and inside was a ring with one lovely, perfect diamond.

Half-joking, Bobby went down on one knee. 'Tina, I'd like us to get married.'

My cold miraculously cured, Bobby and I went off to Nanny Wilde's in Cranbrook Road, me flashing my engagement ring and wearing the mohair outfit despite the fact that it made me look ever so slightly like the Michelin Man.

When we got there, it was to find Nanny Wilde none too pleased because my cousin Danny, Aunt Glad's son and a trainee plumber, had brought round a crowd of his mates from East Ham, uninvited. One of the mates was his best friend David, who had dreams of making it as a celebrity photographer. I vaguely remembered David asking me, two years previously, if I'd let him take some photos of me in Epping Forest. My mother, deeply suspicious of his quite innocent motives, had said, 'Over my dead body.' If she hadn't guarded my virtue so closely, I would now be able to boast of owning a set of portraits of me as a 15-year-old by David Bailey.

By the time we got engaged, Bobby was experiencing his first full season in the first team. For this he was paid £8 a week, which these days wouldn't buy a cheap Alice band for David Beckham. At the time, players were still paid according to the Football League's notorious maximum wage limit of £20 a week during the season and £17 a week in the summer lay-off. That didn't change until 1961, when Jimmy Hill, then a Fulham player and chairman of the Professional Footballers Association, forced through its abolition after threatening a players' strike.

To give an example of how comparatively low foot-ballers' wages were, Bobby's £8 a week was £3 less than I was earning at the Pru, so you could say that I was the breadwinner. Most of our money went into saving like mad for our first home, but life was still a lot of fun. We'd go round in a crowd with the other young West Ham players, like Alan Sealey and Tony Scott, and their girlfriends – Janice, who went out with Alan, was that year's Miss Dagenham and very glamorous. After games we'd go to a private club, Harlene, in Forest Gate, where we girls drank Bristol Cream sherry because we thought it was genteel. Then we'd move on to Room At The Top. Another local hotspot was the Dick Turpin, *the* place to be on Thursday nights. There we'd bump into other young players like Terry Venables and Brian Dear. We used to keep the bar open, but the owners loved us because we were such good customers.

By then, Bobby had bought his first car, a red Ford Zephyr. It was such a momentous occasion that I can still remember its registration number: 2394 PU. A friend of my mother's sold it to him and he paid for it in cash. The transaction took place in Lyons Tea Shop in Ilford, where we had our usual fruit bun with two pats of butter, a bowl of tomato soup and a cup of tea. Bobby arrived with the money in a paper bag. Naturally he had sorted the bills out into denominations first, from pound notes to fifties. They were all in piles facing the right way up and secured with elastic bands. I think he fell short in one way, though – they weren't arranged in numbered sequence.

Bobby loved that Ford Zephyr. It shone, it was immaculate. It was the beginning of his love affair with cars, especially red ones. He was determined to get a Jaguar as soon as he could afford one.

As Bobby became a bit more established in the West Ham team, older players besides Malcolm Allison began to accept him. Chief among them were Johnny Bond and Noel Cantwell. Johnny was known as 'Muffin' after a puppet who featured on a children's TV programme, *Muffin the Mule*. Johnny was alleged to have a kick like the said creature. Noel was nicknamed 'Sausage', which was short for sausage roll and thus meant to rhyme with Noel. Oh, but he was gorgeous. I loved Noel.

Bobby was ravenous for football knowledge and worldly wisdom, so he loved it when the older men included him. He almost sat at their feet. In the first flush of his romance with me, he looked up to them. They represented what he wanted to be.

Malcolm Allison lived a social whirl and during this time he was friendly with a fishmonger's daughter. Bobby and I were invited round to the fishmonger's house one New Year's Eve and after sampling it for the first time in his life, Bobby devoured an entire side of smoked salmon on his own.

It was, after all, the start of the Sixties, when the more luxurious kinds of food were just becoming available after the dreary diet and relative deprivation of the post-war period. We were getting a taste of melon, avocado, French cheese and Italian wine at last. Even broccoli was an exotic luxury to Bobby, as it was to most people in that era. Up to the time I met him, his mum never dished up any vegetables other than the standard staples of those days: peas, cabbage and potatoes.

My mother was very indulgent to me in all sorts of ways, but one thing she was almost draconian about was table manners, as I knew to my cost. When I was young, should I offend, I was despatched from the table. Bobby, who was dazzled by her, set enthusiastically about brushing up his style. He so wanted to be correct in everything he did. He also began to be aware of formal etiquette that he hadn't experienced before, but he really watched and learnt. He was naturally polite and courteous, but now he was adding polish to his manner.

Soon we graduated from the Spaghetti House in Soho. Our next discovery was the 21 Club. Johnny Haynes, Bobby's old childhood hero, introduced us to that. Not only was Johnny very attractive, he had a great personality. He was set to become part of football history – the first player to earn £100. He was captain of England from 1960 to August 1962, when a car accident put him out of the game for a year. It would have made a poignant twist in the tale if Bobby had been his direct replacement as captain, but Jimmy Armfield had a short spell in the job first.

Johnny was also the prototype one-club man. He went on to stay with Fulham for all eighteen years of his career, even though he could have made fortunes more if he had accepted all the opportunities offered to him by other, higher-placed clubs. He was commercially shrewd, though, taking advantage of his brooding, Italianate, Forties film star looks to become an early icon for Brylcreem – with his trademark dark, slicked back hair, he obviously believed in the product he endorsed.

He was a regular at the 21 Club. This was really elegant and exclusive, although the diners sometimes fell short of expectations. Johnny ordered an amazing starter for the three of us – a large silver bowl lined with ice and so full of prawns that they hung over the edge. The prawns were so utterly delicious that as soon as I started eating them, I just got carried away. The next thing I knew, I was looking down at a mountain of empty shells. I couldn't believe I'd eaten so many. I was overcome with remorse. 'Were they very expensive?' I stammered to Johnny.

'Enormously,' said Johnny. 'They're so expensive they have to charge by the prawn.'

'Oh no,' I gasped. 'How do they know how many you've eaten?'

'They count the shells and tails,' said Johnny.

Quickly, I emptied the shells and tails into my handbag. Bobby and Johnny kept straight faces. I had no idea they were winding me up – and did they pull my leg afterwards!

1962 was a big year for us. Bobby turned 21 in April, made his England debut in May and married me in June.

Getting his first full England cap wasn't completely unexpected. He had been doing well in the England Under-23s, which was managed by Ron Greenwood, now his manager at West Ham. Ron was also a good friend of Walter Winterbottom, England team manager at the time, and had been singing Bobby's praises.

In those days it was traditional to have an England v Young England fixture the night before the Cup Final, and

Bobby was pleased with how he'd played because there was still a chance of him making the squad for the 1962 World Cup in Chile. But he'd heard nothing and was resigning himself to go with the rest of the West Ham squad on their close season trip to Africa. Then Ron called him into his office at Upton Park. 'You won't be going on the Africa trip,' he said.

Bobby was startled. He thought he'd done something to offend Ron. Then he saw that Ron was smiling broadly. 'You're off to Chile instead,' he added.

I was absolutely delighted for Bobby. I knew how much it meant to him just to be selected. He warned me not to get my hopes up on his behalf. 'The chances are I'm only there to make up the numbers in training,' he said, 'but at least it'll be good experience for the future.' In fact, he became a fixture in the team from the first match, making his England debut against Peru on 20 May. He was bowled over and so was I. It's every young footballer's dream, and here he was, the man I was about to marry, fulfilling that dream.

Bobby's absence on England duty also gave me the space I needed to organize our wedding with the help of my mother. I'd managed to save around £100 and ended up spending the lot on my wedding dress and accessories. Before the wedding, I had a perm. According to dear mama, it wasn't curly enough, so I was despatched back to the hairdresser to have it re-done. My hair was fine on the day, although later, on honeymoon, Bobby and I had an argument that he won by ducking me in the sea. When I surfaced, I had an Afro.

We were married on 30 June 1962 at St Clement's, Ilford. Noel Cantwell was best man and the Dreaded Eddie gave me away. I wish my mother had given me away herself. After all, she had been mother *and* father to me, she had always been there for me and it was a shame that a man who had come into my life relatively late ended up taking the limelight.

When we arrived at the church after the customary slight delay, I was amazed at the crowd of well-wishers, as well as all the reporters and photographers waiting to pre-serve the bridegroom in his navy mohair suit, white shirt and silk tie for posterity. If I'm honest, I suppose I was rather excited to see them there. All the West Ham team were there and after the ceremony we walked out of the church under an arch of football boots. People plied us with England and West Ham banners along with the more traditional blue garters and black cats. The reception was at the Valentine's public house in Gants Hill. We opened the dancing with 'Blue Moon' – what else?

Afterwards, we were chauffeured to the airport by Budgie Byrne, one of the West Ham lads Bobby used to go gambolling through the night with. It was a wild drive and after being thrown around in the back all the way from Ilford to Heathrow, I staggered into the Skyline Hotel battered and bruised. Bobby and I were starving, so we had beef sandwiches and a pot of tea. I had a white nylon nightie and negligée trimmed with blue daises – looking back, they were revolting. The next day, I changed into my going away outfit, a red Polly Peck suit with a pleated skirt that I'd bought in a sale. Eat your heart out, Victoria Beckham.

We'd booked our honeymoon in Majorca, the Isle of Love. Coincidentally, Malcolm Allison and Noel Cantwell were due to be in Majorca at the same time as us, as my mother was horrified to find out at our wedding reception. 'Look, Tina's only young,' she said, taking Malcolm's arm and drawing him to one side. 'I really do think it would be better if you didn't make any contact with her and Bobby on their honeymoon.'

Malcolm nodded solemnly. A few minutes later, I overheard him telling Bobby, 'I've booked the Astor Club for later.'

It was like a knife through my heart, until I realized he was only joking! Malcolm was a tease.

But my mother was one hundred per cent right about the honeymoon. She knew it would be a disaster if Malcolm and Noel showed their faces in Majorca, because they always led Bobby astray. True to form, they showed up within a week. The three of them got plastered. Bobby was violently sick and spent the night in Noel's room and I ended up sobbing with his wife, Maggie. Can you imagine being on your honeymoon and ending up in bed with the best man's wife while the best man and your husband of one week are together down the corridor?

After we returned home to Gants Hill, Bobby bought me a Hillman Minx for £100, and a Siamese cat. We called it Pele and it quickly became famous when it attacked John Bond. It was a real hard cat, was Pele.

Our first home was a three-bedroomed terrace house in Glenwood Gardens. We'd wanted a slightly grander one nearby but couldn't stretch to the extra £600. It was a shame Brylcreem didn't seek out Bobby's services earlier. Later that year they paid him £450 to appear, with strangely tamped down curls, on an advertising poster. That was a one-off, quite possibly because, unlike Johnny Haynes, Bobby was not a credible Brylcreem man. He didn't have the kind of hair you could slick back. No Brylcreem jar ever graced the bathroom shelf at Glenwood Gardens.

The house had French doors at the back which opened onto a pretty garden where Bobby and I planted a magnolia tree – our favourite. Indoors, the lounge had a green carpet patterned with pink roses and a plate rail going round the walls where we put Bobby's memorabilia.

We were especially proud of our hostess trolley. One Christmas morning, after I'd prepared the turkey and all the trimmings, we went to a drinks party where we met up with our friend Lou Wade. Lou was 6ft 6in tall, thin and Jewish, and he adored Bobby so much that he followed him all over the world. He wore really outlandish clothes and was noted for his garish check jackets, but he was very definitely not a spiv, just an enormous character – his children went to top public schools and his wife was a lady. He used to laugh standing on one leg and he would wind the other leg around it like a snake because he was so tall.

By the time we got back from the Christmas drinks party, Bobby and I were a little bit 'under the weather' and when we went to push the hostess trolley plus contents into the dining room, everything shot onto the floor. We picked up what was salvageable, then rang Lou. 'Bring it round here,' he said, so we had Christmas dinner chez Lou Wade that year.

I suppose that, by today's standards, our Gants Hill house was pretty modest, but Bobby had previously lived in a small house close to an industrial site and I'd had a flat with an outside loo, so to us it was fantastic. Even so, I found the first year of our marriage a bit uncomfortable. It took a long time to adjust to such a huge change in my life. Bobby didn't want me to work, because he trained in the mornings only and came home for lunch. In those days, the close season started in May and stretched on until well into August, so we could get away for lovely long summer holidays. But I missed the company and stimulation of working life at first.

In so many ways, Bobby was a paragon among husbands – I never had to tidy up after him. Not only immaculately dressed, he was also obsessively neat. He just had to arrange everything in order and just so. The clothes in his wardrobe were lined up as though they had been prepared for inspection. His jumpers were hung in sequence from dark to light. It was almost an aesthetic pleasure to open the wardrobe. Something I did find difficult about those early days, though, was that Bobby had been cosseted by his parents, whether it was Big Bob cleaning his muddy boots for him on a Saturday night after the game or Doss's five-star ironing and sewing service. But the incident of the sub-standard Vs in his shorts should have been a warning to me. I had trouble coming up to Doss's standards.

In my own way, I'd been equally spoilt. My mother felt guilty about leaving me to go to work every day and I'd usually be treated to breakfast in bed before she set off. I never ironed. I hadn't really learnt to cook, either, although as my family always ate well, at least I knew how things ought to taste.

After I'd been married for six months, I solved the problem of the ironing. Sometimes I'd visit West Ham to help out in Bobby's sports goods shop. My mother had given up her job as manageress of a large clothes shop to run it for him. It was opposite the stadium in Green Street and one day I took a wander up the road and discovered a Chinese laundry. That was the end of my ironing angst –

I just took everything there from then on. I never let on to Doss, though.

It wasn't only the housework which got me down. In that first year of marriage, Bobby's England career began to take off big time. That, plus his West Ham commitments, meant he was often away. I felt isolated because I'd been used to the warmth and security of Christchurch Road, with Auntie Mum, Uncle Jim and my three cousins, Marlene, Jenny and Jimmy, just a flight of stairs away.

A while before I got married, Auntie Mum and her family had moved to Barkingside, so I reverted to the bosom of my family, driving round there in my Hillman Minx, Pele in his cat basket beside me. It meant I could spend time with my cousin Jimmy, to whom I'd always been close. Although Jimmy wasn't much older than me, he was now more or less housebound. He had been doing his National Service when he came home for a spell on leave and started staggering when he walked. Soon he couldn't even carry his bike indoors. Uncle Jim thought he was malingering because he didn't want to go back to the Army, but the reality was much, much worse; he was diagnosed with multiple sclerosis.

Jimmy suffered from a particularly virulent form of the disease and he wasn't with us for much longer. After he died, Bobby helped me to organize an auction of West Ham and England autographed memorabilia, which made enough to buy and adapt a transport van for MS sufferers to use, so at least Jimmy's death resulted in some benefit to others.

It was after the World Cup in Chile that Bobby's fame really started to spread. By the end of 1962, Walter Winterbottom had decided to stand down as England manager and Alf Ramsey, who replaced him, made it clear from very early on that he saw Bobby as his future captain. Alf was quiet, self-controlled and introverted. He also knew exactly what he wanted and I think he saw his mirror image in Bobby. England's first game under Alf was against France in the European Championships. England were beaten 5–2, but Bobby came back full of the joys because Alf had actually sat down next to him as the team bus was leaving Paris. 'He was asking me all sorts of questions about the team under Walter and where I thought I should play,' marvelled Bobby. 'I get the idea he's really going to sort things out.'

In spite of the fact that Bobby was young and relatively new to the team, Alf made him captain within a few months of that France defeat, against Czechoslovakia on 12 May 1963 – Bobby's twelfth cap. Bobby revelled in leading the side out in front of the fanatically partisan crowd in Bratislava. England won 4–2 and the big occasion inspired him to a performance that brought rave reviews from the English press.

I had to wrestle with my feelings about Bobby's

increasing fame. On the one hand I was thrilled for him that things were going so well. On the other hand, now everybody wanted to be Bobby Moore's friend. That was a little difficult to deal with at first. Before we got married, we'd been an ordinary courting couple. Having the press at our wedding and all those strangers crowding around to wish us well had been lovely, but beyond that it really hadn't occurred to me that we'd be in the public eye all the time and what that would entail.

I'd been used to having Bobby to myself more or less one hundred per cent and, naively, thought that was how it would continue. Now the hangers-on were starting to appear. I was actually quite taken aback when we kept getting interrupted while we were out for a quiet dinner.

Through friends we met one Stanley Flashman, king of ticket touts and future owner of Barnet FC, where he achieved legendary status by employing Barry Fry as manager, then sacking and re-instating him almost on a weekly basis at one stage. Stan's industrial-sized figure made him instantly recognizable. He would come up with tickets and backstage passes to all the top shows and introduce us to a whole host of people who then invited us to parties, weddings, bar mitzvahs . . . you name it. Some of those events were great. Others, where it would turn out that Bobby was the prize exhibit and used for photo opportunities, were a pain. He caught on to it soon enough. He hated letting people down and was never, ever abrupt or rude, but he had a way of withdrawing behind a wall of politeness if necessary.

I loved the real fans. They were wonderful. What I didn't like was the idea of Bobby being exploited by people for their own benefit, or used and taken advantage of. I was protective of him. In fact, we had an understanding: when it got too much for him, he would give me a special look. Very soon after, I would rush up to him and say, 'Oh! Bobby, don't forget we've got to . . .' and then produce some fictitious commitment which meant we had to leave *tout de suite*. Then we would head off somewhere where we knew we wouldn't be disturbed, like the White Elephant Club. Bobby's party trick there was to stand behind the bar, seemingly innocuously. It was only if you looked behind the bar that you would see he had his trousers down.

Totally out of character for the dignified, self-controlled Bobby Moore? Not a bit of it. It's a thing young men do. It wasn't even terribly naughty. Mind you, he did keep his boxer shorts on.

It was around this time, incidentally, that Bobby's existence was noted by the world of high fashion. The September 1962 issue of *Vogue* pictured him in his West Ham strip, surrounded by four gorgeous models. The rest of the world was discovering what I already knew – that Bobby Moore was beautiful as well as brilliant. And soon he would prove that he was brave as well.

CHAPTER FIVE

A Light Grey

Bobby's yelp of pain jerked me wide awake. Slowly, because I was heavily pregnant, I sat up and switched on the lamp. 'Bobby, what's the matter?' I said.

I already had the answer. Lying next to me, he was doubled up. I went cold with fear. 'Please, Bobby, you can't leave it any longer,' I said. 'You've got to get it seen.'

It was November 1964. Bobby's career was on a roll. Earlier in the year, he had been elected Footballer of the Year by the Football Writers Association and two days after accepting the award, he had led West Ham to their first FA Cup victory at Wembley. We were expecting our first child in January and both of us were absolutely thrilled at the prospect. And then this.

He had noticed the lump in his testicle a few weeks earlier. The discovery had alarmed him and he'd mentioned it to the club physio, but between them they decided it was a sports injury, caused when someone kicked him in a tender place during training. It would probably disappear of its own accord in a couple of weeks. Until then, it wasn't worth bothering the doctor. But it didn't disappear. Instead, it became more and more painful until, turning over in bed that night and jarring it with the extra weight of my pregnant body, I put him in agony. Something was obviously badly wrong.

The next morning, at the GP's surgery, we saw our family doctor. Dr Kennedy was one of life's true gentlemen and a dedicated physician who really pulled out all the stops for us. Instead of going home to Gants Hill with me, Bobby was sent straight to the London Hospital. Within twenty-four hours, he was on the operating table.

As soon as he came round, he had a nurse ring me up. She handed him the phone. 'I just want to tell you, I love you,' he said.

I sighed with relief. I'd had such a horrible, despondent feeling about the operation. 'Everything's going to be fine,' I thought.

When I went to visit him at the hospital that evening, I expected to be told he'd be well enough to come home within a few days. I hadn't even got as far as Bobby's bed when the consultant called me into his office. 'I'm afraid we found cancer,' he said.

The consultant's name was Mr Tresidder. I questioned the poor man over and over and he did his best to comfort and reassure me. 'There are all kinds of tumours,' he said.

A Light Grey

'They come in all shades from grey to black, and Bobby's was a light grey.'

I tried to concentrate on what he was telling me, but I was so frightened for Bobby that I could barely make sense of the words. In that situation, you don't hear anything except the word you don't want to hear. *Cancer, cancer, cancer.*

'Don't tell Bobby that's what it is,' I begged him.

From the beginning to the end of his treatment, Bobby and I never once mentioned the C word. I kept on asking the consultant questions; I must have driven him to distraction. I also went to the library and read up as much as I could about it, although the books weren't very informative. I wanted to know every angle, every possibility. Most of all, I didn't want Bobby to know. I thought it would really crush him and badly affect his chances of recovery.

Looking back, Bobby must have realized what was wrong with him. He wasn't stupid and besides, he had great courage. Even if Mr Tresidder had skirted round the issue, I'm convinced that Bobby would have put two and two together and pressed him for the truth. What's more, not only do I think he was aware what the problem was but I'm pretty sure he'd made a mental vow not to disclose it to me because he wanted to protect me. All he said to me about it was, 'Don't tell anyone what I'm in here for.'

I was frantic with worry. I didn't know how long he'd

had it. I was 22. At that sort of age, you tend to believe you're immortal. Cancer just isn't something you think about. Up until then, our lives had been full of fun and success. Now I didn't know whether he'd live or die, let alone if he'd ever be able to play football again. I didn't know how any of it would affect him mentally, or how I would cope.

These days young men are much more aware of testicular cancer and the importance of checking regularly for signs. People talk about it openly, without shame or embarrassment. When Lance Armstrong won the Tour de France for the first time, everyone knew he had conquered this disease just a few years earlier. He was not only a sporting hero but someone who had confronted and defied the most terrifying of illnesses at an age when most of his contemporaries thought they were at death's door if they had a heavy cold.

But cancer was a taboo word in the Sixties. We were years away from the internet with its numerous medical websites that would help de-mystify the disease. The only thing someone like me knew about cancer was that it was very likely to kill you. All I could think about was, 'Bobby's only 23 and he's been handed his death warrant. And I'm just about to have his baby.'

I think the night the consultant told me what was wrong was the worst of my life. Although I had been baptized a Catholic, I had never been very religious. Even so, that night I felt so scared and alone that I went to see a priest. I desperately needed to disclose this awful thing to someone and, at the time, breaking the news to Doss and Big Bob or my mother, all people who loved him more than the world, was completely beyond me.

After I told the priest, I kept my vow of silence as long as I could. It lasted a week. Then my mother came to stay. I was in such a state she slept in my bed. I couldn't stop sobbing.

'Tina, what's wrong?' She kept pressing gently for an answer.

In the end I cracked and told her. It was awful for her, too. She absolutely adored Bobby. By then he'd taken over the little sports goods shop opposite the West Ham stadium and turned it into Bobby Moore Ltd. My mother had given up her job to run it for him and they really got on. They were friends and colleagues, not just mother- and son-in-law.

She was the only person I told for ages. I couldn't even bring myself to confide at that stage in Judith Hurst, someone I would have trusted completely not to tell anyone else, not even Geoff. Why burden her? What could you say to anybody? What could anybody do?

'You're not to worry, Bobby. The team's playing fine and Martin Peters is doing very well in your place.'

Martin Peters is doing what? Bristling, I sneaked a glance at Ron Greenwood from under my eyelashes. What on earth did the man think he was up to, telling Bobby how well West Ham were doing without him?

I'd really dressed up to the nines to visit Bobby that day. I was wearing high-heeled boots and a coat of my mother's which had a big fox fur collar. It was far too mature and sophisticated an outfit for me – I probably looked like lamb dressed as mutton – but I felt marvellous. I was determined to look good for Bobby. He was worrying about me because I was seven months pregnant and I wanted him to know I could cope.

And now Ron Greenwood had to come out with that.

I could see the effect it had had on Bobby. He was smiling blandly in acknowledgement, but his eyes had glazed over. That told me all I needed to know about his exasperation, anger, fear and despair.

I thought, 'Ron, you might be a fantastic manager and a wonderful coach, but you have no idea how to handle people.' How could he say such a thing to a young man who had just had a testicle removed, whose whole life was playing football and who had just been told he had a tumour? Surely he must have known what a sensitive issue it was. Because of Bobby's profession, he was extra vulnerable. What had happened struck at his livelihood, his masculinity and his very existence on the planet. But where Ron should have been compassionate, his first thought was for the team – and he assumed Bobby thought the same.

Ron and Bobby had a strange relationship. Ron first

marked him out as a future star when Bobby was playing for the England Under-23 team. In the same way that he did with Malcolm Allison, Bobby used to follow him around like a hungry puppy, pestering him with questions about strategy and technique. He really admired Ron's tactical knowledge. For a while this man was, to Bobby, the fount of all football wisdom.

And Ron admired him right back. He liked to say that one of the main reasons he agreed to leave Arsenal to take on the manager's job at West Ham was because Bobby was there and he would be able to build the side round him. But the relationship began to turn sour over their disputes about salary increases. Even then, the amounts involved were so petty that I felt the disputes weren't really about money at all, but control. Bobby wanted to be acknowledged for what he was worth, but Ron couldn't or wouldn't see that. He had no idea how to handle Bobby. He'd known him for years and yet it was as though he'd absorbed absolutely no information about Bobby as a human being at all.

He was obviously trying to cheer Bobby up, but telling him how well West Ham were doing without him was hardly the shot in the arm he needed. Ron went about it in completely the wrong way. What Bobby needed to hear from his manager was, 'Bobby, we're missing you! We need our captain back!'

Of course it wasn't deliberate. Ron wasn't trying to

put Bobby in his place or cut him down to size. He just didn't have the necessary empathy. The interpersonal skills weren't there. When I first met Ron's wife, Lucy, practically her opening remark was 'Ron lives and breathes football' and as an assessment of his personality and interests, that was spot on. Ron was someone, I felt, who put football before everything else.

I really don't mean this to be disrespectful to him. Ron Greenwood never did anything to hurt me personally. He was a good man, a very moral man, scrupulous and decent. But with those qualities also came an intensity that made him find lots of things in this life superfluous. He couldn't be bothered with what he regarded as trivial. It was beyond him that the lads wanted to have fun by going out drinking and having a good time rather than sitting at home night after night thinking about 4-2-4.

I also think that as the years progressed, there was a certain degree of jealousy or resentment in his feelings towards Bobby. Nearly forty years later, when Sir Alex Ferguson and David Beckham fell out, it was as if history was repeating itself. Here were two managers who felt they had created their players to a certain degree and neither of them could deal with what he'd created – a charismatic, fashionable player who was getting larger than the club, an alpha football star. When Bobby was elected Footballer of the Year, the youngest ever at 23, Ron refused to let anyone from the club go to the Café Royal to support him. He said it was because it was too close to the Cup Final. That really hurt and disappointed Bobby. The barriers went up.

Ron was never anything but courteous to me, but he didn't exude great warmth. As Bobby's wife, I had never really been able to understand why they couldn't communicate better when they both ultimately wanted the same thing – success for West Ham. After that episode at the hospital, I realized why Bobby felt the way he did and I was sorry that Ron wasn't able to look below the surface and take into account Bobby's fear and vulnerability.

When Bobby came home from hospital, all we seemed to do was cry. We would cling together on the sofa in front of the television, watching *Top Of The Pops* with tears streaming down our faces. He was so desolate. When they'd had to remove the affected testicle, it was as though, in his mind, they'd taken his manhood away with it. The first time we went on holiday after the operation, buying shorts was an ordeal for him. He was very self-conscious, thinking people could see what was wrong. He worried that it looked unsightly and he didn't feel whole.

The routine details of a footballer's life made things even tougher for him. Other men could conceal such a personal thing, but in the dressing room and communal bath it was terribly difficult to hide anything. After he left hospital, he had to go back as an outpatient for radiotherapy. Blue crosses had to be drawn on his back to show the position of his kidneys so the radiotherapist could avoid them. He was out of the game for three months.

Did the senior people at West Ham know what was wrong? I'm sure one or two had their private suspicions, but nothing was ever said to me or Bobby. Neither was there any speculation in the press about the cause of Bobby's long lay-off. Not a single journalist asked Bobby or me about it. Hard to believe in an era when David Beckham's broken metatarsal can make front page news, but in those days it wasn't automatic for clubs to divulge health information. The explanation that Bobby was suffering from a severe groin injury satisfied the gentlemen of the press.

It didn't filter down to Bobby's team-mates, either. All they knew about it was that he'd had to go into hospital for a course of treatment. Bobby, guarded and reserved by nature, became almost paranoid about the other lads seeing the big blue Xs marking the spot whenever he took off his shirt. He became a master of evasion, only getting into the communal bath when he was on his own. He would pretend to be busy with something else until the others had got out. What a trial that must have been to him.

For five years after the operation he had to undergo regular check-ups. That caused him endless worry and, not surprisingly, every ache and pain, however niggling, terrified him – and me.

A Light Grey

How we got through the early weeks after his illness I can't explain. It was very tough, but I think we were both the kind of people who believe in the power of positive thinking. By then I'd found out enough about his illness from Mr Tresidder and from my research at the library to know that Bobby stood a good chance of a normal life. The best way of dealing with it just seemed to be to get on with it. Besides, the fact that our baby was going to arrive any day soon gave Bobby something happy and life-affirming to think about. He was going to be a father. He couldn't fall apart.

I was anxious for him, of course. Who wouldn't have been? At night I'd fall asleep as usual, then wake a few hours later with my heart pounding in panic. The other half of the bed would be unoccupied. I'd go round the house looking for him. Either he'd be downstairs in his pyjamas, pacing the floor, or fully dressed, having just come in from walking around the streets in the middle of the night.

All the press wrote later about him being a chronic insomniac. That was when it started.

Roberta Christina Moore was born on 24 January 1965, while the father-to-be performed the traditional role of pacing the corridor outside the delivery room. If any one good thing came out of those hellish months, it was her doing.

They do say that a baby is wired to reflect the emotional

81

state of its mother. I had been living in turmoil since November. The birth had been really difficult, too. 'Congratulations,' the midwife had said to me. 'It's my first baby, too.'

'That doesn't come as any surprise to me at all,' I would have said, if I hadn't been too exhausted to speak. I felt ripped to pieces – and indeed had been, thanks to that midwife. She might as well have been wearing an L plate on the back of her overall.

I absolutely adored Roberta from the moment I saw her. She was gorgeous and tiny and perfect. My love for her was overwhelming, but the trauma over Bobby's illness threw everything out of kilter. Roberta was so little and new, but she must have arrived with some kind of internal tuning fork. She picked everything up. She was fractious. She didn't want to eat. She wouldn't sleep. Just like her daddy. In fact, she was shaping up to be the archetypal Moore.

Bobby was wonderful with her and he welcomed the distraction. She wasn't spoilt, but she was a strong-willed personality even then. Often, when I woke in the night, I'd find him downstairs, feeding or changing her. That's if either of them were around at all! Sometimes they were out together – he'd be driving her around in the back of the car to get her to settle.

The two of them formed an unbelievably strong bond. To this day, I think Roberta regards him as the ideal man.

*   *   *

Bobby was back in training by the end of February and I got on with adjusting to motherhood. My mother came round one day and found me on my hands and knees as I washed the kitchen floor. 'Get up,' she said, 'I didn't bring you up to do this.' She waited until Bobby came back, then told him, 'Tina needs help.'

I heartily agreed with her. We phoned an au pair agency and Sophia joined the household in Gants Hill. I was 22 and she was 27, with long, black hair and stunning looks that stopped the Ilford traffic. When we went out, she pushed the Marmet pram and I clung on to the edge, like the child.

'I wouldn't have employed her,' said one friend of mine after another. 'She's too attractive.'

'She can look like Sophia Loren and Liz Taylor rolled into one for all I care,' I laughed. 'She's fabulous with kids and totally trustworthy, and that's all that matters.'

The most important thing was that Bobby's football hadn't been affected by his illness. In May he captained West Ham to a 2–0 win in the European Cup Winners' Cup against TSV Munich 1860 at Wembley. We'd had a nightmare no one knew about and now we were waking up from it. Life was for living again.

We wanted to thank Dr Kennedy for everything he'd done for us, so Bobby gave him one of his England shirts. Dr Kennedy was also a lay preacher at the Congregational Church in Buckhurst Hill, Essex, and he took the shirt with him next time he had to give a sermon. He held it up in front of the congregation. 'Do you know what this is?'

'It's an England shirt,' piped up a very small boy.

Dr Kennedy turned it round to show the Number Six on the back. 'And do you know who wore this shirt?' he asked him.

'Bobby Moore.'

After that, he returned to the main subject. 'Do you know who God is?' he asked.

Easy one, that. 'Bobby Moore,' said the boy.

CHAPTER SIX

Happy Days

'Bobby . . . I'm pregnant.'

His face just lit up. It was never something he would talk about, but I know that after his treatment for testicular cancer he was worried about his fertility, even though he'd been told it wouldn't be affected. So when I became pregnant again, towards the end of 1966, I was thrilled. We wanted another child anyway because we got so much out of being parents to Roberta, but this also went a long way to allaying Bobby's worries about whether he was still a 'whole man'.

Soon after, though, I had a miscarriage. That cast a cloud over what should have been an exciting time, because Bobby was awarded an OBE in the New Year's Honours List of 1 January 1967. We told ourselves that it was probably for the best as there might have been something wrong with the baby, but that in itself brought back a lot of the uncertainties. That's why Dean's birth, fourteen months on, was such a cause for celebration.

By then we had left our Gants Hill semi to live in Chigwell, an affluent suburb in Essex's stockbroker belt. The mock Tudor house in Manor Road cost £11,000 and was detached, with four bedrooms and a lovely, homely feel about it. Roberta, who was two at the time of the move, has incredibly happy memories of that house. So do Dean and I. It was the backdrop to the really golden days.

Dean was born on 24 March 1968. That was a Saturday and Bobby had got me tickets for West Ham's home game against Chelsea. The wonderful Dr Kennedy, who had seen us through the horrible weeks of Bobby's illness, came with me in case Dean decided to make his debut at Upton Park.

It was a good thing the doctor was there. I started having twinges shortly before kick-off. I got out of the ground and headed for Bobby's shop across the road while someone got word to Bobby. Dean's imminent arrival then became the post-match entertainment, with Bobby hurriedly changing out of his West Ham strip and him and Dr Kennedy escorting me to a car through a huge crush of fans shouting, 'Go on, Teen!' and 'Good on you, girl!'

Bobby was with me, holding my hand, throughout the birth and when Dean was born, healthy and perfect, he couldn't hold back the tears as he held his son for the first time. We both cried. I knew how much this meant to him. It was such an emotionally charged moment, the ultimate proof that his fears were unfounded and that he had totally

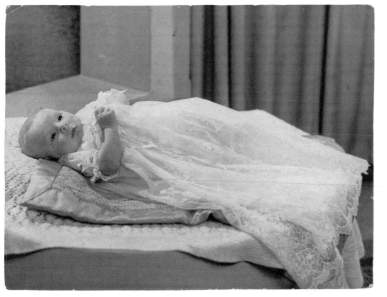

A star is born.

The makings of an Adonis. Bobby at the beach, aged 10.

'Any girl who gets My Robert into trouble will have me to deal with.' Doss with five-year-old Bobby, her only child.

Right: My beautiful mother, Betty. We'd walk down the road together and men would whistle at her, not me.

Right: My grandmother, Nanny Wilde, whom I adored. I used to go round to her house to listen to her play the piano and sing.

Above: Part of mummy's grooming plans. Tina in jodhpurs at Christchurch Road.

Above: Wilde women: (left to right) Aunt Glad (married to Jimmy), Aunt Eileen, Aunt Molly ('Auntie Mum'), Betty, Aunt Kit, Aunt Glad II, and Aunt Edna.

Love's young dream. Bobby and I at our engagement party at Nanny Wilde's,
Christmas Day 1960.

Before he was famous. Bobby as a West Ham colt, with Andy Smillie (left) and
Tony Swift.

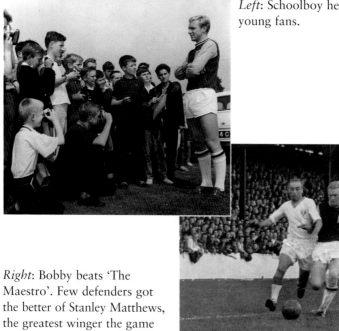

Left: Schoolboy hero. Bobby with some young fans.

Right: Bobby beats 'The
Maestro'. Few defenders got
the better of Stanley Matthews,
the greatest winger the game
has ever seen.

Above: Mr and Mrs Bobby Moore.

Left: Lovely dress, shame about the carpet. With my mother on my wedding day, 30 June 1962.

West Ham girls on their way to Wembley: (from left) Mrs Boyce, Hurst, Burkett, Brown, Standen, Brabrook and Moore.

Right and below: Hammers Fly High! Bobby celebrating West Ham's 1964 FA Cup final win with Johnny Byrne.
Chin up! Ron Greenwood leads the team out at Wembley, with captain Bobby ahead of Johnny Byrne, Eddie Bovington and John Bond.

Above: Glory day. Bobby with the cup aloft after the 3–2 win against Preston NE at Wembley.

Above: 'We're forever blowing bubbles'. West Ham's first FA Cup trophy was soon followed by Bobby being nominated Footballer of the Year.

Above: Local heroes. Celebrating with the fans in an open-top bus parade of the East End, following their Wembley triumph.

Left: Alan Sealey, Brian Dear, and Bobby with the 1965 European Cup Winner's Cup trophy.

Below: Proud mum and dad. Big Bob and Doss showing off their son's growing collection of trophies.

Above: Our first holiday together, Italy 1959. Obviously preparing for future dramas at sea . . .

Right: Mean, moody and magnificent.

defeated the cancer. 'You look so beautiful,' he whispered to me, 'the best you've ever looked.'

Dean was such a good baby, unbelievably happy and contented. I couldn't believe we were so blessed. In the mornings Bobby would be awake before everyone else, bringing me tea and preparing Dean's feed. He loved to give Dean his early morning bottle. It was a chance to spend time alone with Dean and bond with him the way he'd done with Roberta.

Our home life was actually quite ordinary and mundane most of the time, in a lovely way. Every Saturday before a game I'd cook Bobby a steak, and at dinner I'd put candles on the table and serve avocado and some hopeful attempt at cordon bleu. On weekdays Bobby would often be at home in the afternoons, so he would take the little ones to the park to feed the ducks or play on the swings.

He wanted to have a normal father-child relationship with them and played it down when people approached him for his autograph or pointed him out. He hated it when once Roberta, aged six, went to a friend's house and the dad said, 'What's it like having Bobby Moore as a father?' It just seemed such a bizarre question, coming from another dad. She was really puzzled by the way he stopped and looked at her searchingly, waiting for the answer. Bobby wondered what he expected Roberta to say. To the children he was their father and that was his most important role, not Bobby Moore the footballer.

It didn't always matter if people didn't actually know us. Some still entertained the fantasy that they did. Soon after we moved into our new house, I was at a restaurant in Chigwell with a girlfriend when I overheard someone at an adjacent table say, 'Bobby Moore lives here. I met his wife the other day.'

'Oh, really?' someone else said. 'What was she like?'

I had never, ever, set eyes on those people in my life.

Roberta, Dean and I used to go to Upton Park for home games, where we'd sit in the same three seats immediately behind the Directors' Box every time. Bobby developed a secret wave for the children as he ran onto the pitch, one hand under the opposing armpit and wiggling his fingers. During half-time and after the game, we would be banished to a little room designated the Wives' Lounge, where we were given Mother's Pride sandwiches, cupcakes and custard creams and would sit there docilely, having a chit-chat while the men got on with doing the business. Only on certain big occasions were we allowed into the Directors' Lounge. There we'd be offered wine, gin and tonic and prawn sandwiches – much more like it.

One of my fondest memories is of Christmas, when Bobby would take Roberta and Dean to Upton Park to watch while he and the lads worked off the seasonal excesses to hone themselves for the Boxing Day game. The Irish groundsman, known with great originality as Paddy, liked a drink. Around Christmas he always needed help keeping the white lines straight and sometimes they looked particularly artistic, especially when he allowed Master Dean to help him paint them. Meanwhile, Miss Roberta would be industriously sweeping the stands in her party dress.

In the late Sixties and Seventies, there were no such things as executive boxes at Upton Park. It was long before the Taylor Report, which led to all-seater stadiums being introduced for safety reasons. In those days we still had the Chicken Run, an area opposite the main stand to the right of the Directors' Box. No seats, and the back row was used as an impromptu *pissoir* so it wasn't the sweetest-smelling place in the world, but it teemed with the most fervent, supportive, good-humoured fans. Bobby loved them and you could often catch the smile on his face after some witty remark from one of the crowd. The whole place was great. It had a lovely, familiar feel. It wasn't slick and business-orientated like it is now.

And, of course, we were in the prime of our lives, with young children and lots of friends and a standard of living that earlier generations of footballers had never dreamed of, thanks to England's World Cup victory, and we wanted to make the most of it. Most of the West Ham team seemed to have their children at around the same time and life was full of christenings and Sunday morning drinks and birthday parties and bonfire nights and barbies.

Often after a game Bobby and I would head for the Black Lion in Plaistow to meet up with Harry Redknapp, Frankie Lampard and their wives, two pretty sisters called Sandra and Pat. They were very alike, with high, chiselled cheekbones and lovely, down-to-earth personalities. The similarity didn't end there as both went on to produce sons who carried on the family football tradition – Jamie Redknapp and Frankie Lampard Junior. Bobby and I would also regularly have dinner with Geoff and Judith Hurst and Lisa and Jim Standen.

All Bobby's football buddies used to come round – Geoff Hurst, Martin Peters, Harry Redknapp and Brian Dear from West Ham, Rodney Marsh of Queens Park Rangers, Frank McLintock of Arsenal. Later on, after he signed for the Gunners in 1971, Alan Ball was almost part of the furniture. In fact, Dean has a distinct recollection of Alan standing on a chair, with glass in hand and singing lustily, at one of our parties.

Roberta and Dean looked on them all as a big bunch of uncles. Dean's christening party became so uproarious that a policeman drew up outside in a Morris Minor and knocked at the door to tell us that one of the neighbours had complained about the noise. Bobby invited him in and within minutes his hat was off and he was dancing around the lounge with the wife of West Ham physio Rob Jenkins. He stayed for about two hours.

Dean's godfather was John 'Budgie' Byrne, one of those

bubbly, prankster-ish characters who so attracted Bobby, like Noel Cantwell and Harry Redknapp. The explanation for his nickname was simple – he talked so much. Before he joined West Ham, his great claim to fame was that he was one of the last players to win an England cap while with a Third Division side, Crystal Palace. Bobby's friendship with Budgie was forged very early on and never wavered – he was someone Bobby could relax with and he was enormously loyal. He wasn't looking for reflected glory or anything other than friendship and the whole family loved him and Margaret, his wife. He had first claim on our sofa if he couldn't make it home after a long evening out.

That doesn't mean that Budgie was The One – Bobby's best buddy. In all the years I knew him, Bobby never had one particular friend, no one of whom, if someone asked me, I could say, 'So-and-so was Bobby's real mate' – whatever that person thought or said themselves. I was struck by that from when I first met him. He didn't keep in touch with any school friends.

That emotional distance from other males was just Bobby's nature. He liked everybody, to a greater or lesser degree. Some he admired particularly or had a great fondness for and some he got on especially well with, like Terry Creasey, who was a huge West Ham supporter and had big brown eyes magnified even more by his glasses, which he was always pushing back from the tip of his nose like

Eric Morecambe. He liked Les Strong of Fulham and Alan Ball, too. He and Geoff Hurst held each other in mutual respect, but they never had the close personal friendship that Judith and I shared. Bobby wasn't a man who had that deep 'buddy buddy' thing with other men – he had a reserve. I don't think that attitude was peculiar to Bobby, either – not all men have deep friendships the way women do. Bobby loved me and his children, and friends were peripheral to that.

Even so, these friends were always in our lives. Football was a much smaller world then. Overseas signings were virtually unheard of. Boys like Bobby, Geoff and Martin grew up in the same area and came from the same working-class background. Even after clubs lost their powers to dictate whether or not a player could leave, many players expected to spend most of their professional careers with just one or two clubs. There still wasn't the big money to be made from transfers. These days, it just wouldn't happen. Football teams aren't made up mainly of local lads any more. Multi-million pound signings from all over the country and from other parts of the world live the life of movie stars. They're protected by agents and hide behind electronically operated gates with security cameras. For some it's one season, perhaps two, at a club, then time to move on.

Forty years on, Judith Hurst and I are still friends. Even although Bobby is gone, and my life is very different now,

I have kept many of the friends that he and I made when he was starting out in football. Maybe I'm wrong, but I don't think it's so easy for footballers and their families to make lifelong friendships any more.

Our au pairs were lovely girls, part of the family. Bobby was away so often that I really appreciated their companionship. It didn't take me long to adapt to having what might be called 'staff'. The first one, Sophia, who was about a foot taller and five years older, ordered me around most efficiently and after that I was housebroken.

One of the au pairs who passed through our lives was Frankie, from Germany. She was quite a big girl. One night when Bobby and I were out, Frankie tripped over upstairs and got herself jammed between the bed and the wall. She was in a lot of pain, so the ever-resourceful and organized Roberta, aged six, went downstairs and looked up the GP's number in the book. The GP arrived and rang for an ambulance and, as Frankie couldn't remember where we had gone, he took Roberta and Dean to his house, together with Bubbles, the white Persian cat. Roberta refused to leave it behind.

Bobby and I didn't get home until three in the morning, but as usual we looked in on the children. Bobby had had a few but I heard him say, 'Goodnight, Dean,' and meanwhile I looked into Roberta's room. Her bed was empty. I went into Dean's room, wondering if she had crept in there, but not only was she missing – so was Dean. Bobby had said goodnight to a toy.

Eventually, after running all over the house, we found a note from the GP explaining what had happened. It was funny in retrospect, but in fact later on we would have had every reason to panic. Not long after we got home from the World Cup in Mexico in June 1970 someone sent an anonymous letter, postmarked Birmingham, to the *London Evening Standard* warning of a plot to kidnap me and the children. The writer, an ex-con, claimed to be a big fan of Bobby's but couldn't give his name because the police wanted his help with their enquiries on another matter. But, he said, he'd heard from underworld sources that five men, two of them armed, were involved. They were planning to demand a ransom of £10,000.

The *Evening Standard* rang the police. They contacted Ron Greenwood at West Ham straightaway. It was pretty dramatic, because the team was about to head off for a pre-season friendly against Bournemouth. The team bus was actually standing in the Upton Park forecourt when Bobby was tapped on the shoulder and told what was happening. When Bobby saw the letter, he had a strong feeling it was authentic. People sent him crank letters now and again, but this one was legible and rational. It added up. He took his bag off the bus and came home. The police took the letter seriously, too. They posted a 24-hour watch on our house at the front, the back and inside, which meant a total of nine detectives, working in threes in eight-hour shifts. I even had a policeman to carry my basket when I went shopping. I could have got used to that.

It took us a couple of days to become accustomed to them answering the front door for us and listening in on the phone extension, but after that they just became part of the family. They played cards and watched television with us; and it cost Bobby a fortune in lager! At the time we had an English girl, Pauline, working for us as a mother's help. She was a lovely, tender, gentle person who spoke with a soft Suffolk burr. The first evening the detectives were there, Pauline and I were in the kitchen watching them playing with the kids in the garden when I pointed to one of them. 'He looks really nice,' I said. 'I've got a funny feeling you're going to marry him.'

I must have been psychic. Roberta was a bridesmaid at their wedding, secretly swigging sherry, mob cap over one eye. Bobby gave one of the speeches. 'While the bridegroom was stopping someone making off with one of our family,' he said, 'he went and kidnapped our nanny.'

Not long after the foiling of the kidnap plot, Bobby received a death threat. It came via a phone call received by my cousin Jenny as she minded the sports shop opposite the ground. 'Bobby's going to be shot,' said the caller, who declined to identify himself.

The call actually came through while a match was taking place, so Jenny rang the police and they sent a squad car hurtling round to Upton Park, where they waited until the referee blew for time. Then they advanced on Bobby and surrounded him.

'I know I wasn't that great today, but I didn't think Ron would have me arrested,' he joked as they escorted him off the pitch.

'Yeah, sorry about this,' one of them replied. 'It's just that your wife's cousin got a phone call saying someone was going to shoot you from the stands.'

'Well, if they tried, they must be a worse shot than me,' Bobby said.

No one was ever charged with either the kidnap plot or the death threat, but the damage had been done. For a while I became ultra-security conscious to the point of paranoia, frightened to let the kids outside. If Roberta and Dean went anywhere without us, Bobby and I would fret until they came home. Things like that weren't just scary to live through, they altered your mindset.

Once, in an interview with a reporter, I commented that it was sometimes a hard life. The journalist made fun of me – 'Yeah, right.' But it wasn't a normal life. Yes, we had all the material trappings but they didn't make us invulnerable. Receiving crank letters was just irritating most of the time, but these threats to harm us were credible and absolutely harrowing.

The bad had to be accepted along with the good. The 1966

World Cup had proved to be a turning point financially. It was a wonderful time to be young, blond and captain of England, although even then, Bobby had to go into battle with Ron Greenwood.

Their first pay fight had taken place in 1961, when the maximum wage was abolished. Bobby was on £20 a week by then but he felt he was worth £30. While the rest of the West Ham first team settled for £28, Bobby hung out for the extra £2. Six weeks of violent disagreement about a relatively trivial sum of money ended when the club put everyone's weekly wages up to £30 so the whole business could be settled.

Bobby had to do all his own pay bargaining because the Football League refused to let agents act for players in contract negotiations. So he would find himself in the ludicrous situation of arguing with Ron about money in the afternoon, then have to co-operate with him at training the next day. That was how the English game was run then, with a manager having to double up as coach and businessman. It hurt Bobby's working relationship with Ron, which was damaged again in 1966 during England's World Cup preparations, after Bobby was secretly approached by Spurs. He relayed the news to Ron. It was inevitable that Ron dug in his heels. 'West Ham won't let you go under any circumstances,' he said.

'At the very least I should get a pay rise for staying,' said Bobby.

'I'm not going to discuss it any more,' said Ron. 'It can wait until the World Cup's over.'

Bobby said that was fine by him, but Ron brooded about it and became more and more outraged. Finally, he unburdened himself to a journalist. To Bobby's displeasure, the pay discussions that he had thought were secret found their way into the papers.

Bobby was every bit as stubborn as Ron. His current contract with West Ham was due to expire on 30 June and he refused to sign a new one. After that, he would no longer be officially contracted to any club in the Football League, which would mean that he wouldn't legally exist as a player in the eyes of the FA. This was rather a dubious position for him to be in, considering he was about to lead England into the World Cup Finals.

'You've got to regularize your position,' Alf Ramsey told him at Hendon Hall, the England team hotel. 'Just sign a contract for one month – long enough for you to play in the Final. Then Alf turned his attention to Ron Greenwood. 'Get round here immediately and sort this thing out,' he ordered.

When an abashed Ron arrived, Bobby was waiting for him in the foyer.

Alf pointed to a private office off the foyer. 'The two of you . . . in there. You've got one minute. Then I want you out of here, Ron.'

Ron and Bobby did as they were told.

Happy Days

After the World Cup, Bobby was in a much stronger position when he returned to Upton Park. This time he negotiated a rise which nearly doubled his pay to £150. In return, he signed a three-year contract with West Ham holding an option to keep him for three more years after that. It probably didn't compare with what Bobby Charlton and Georgie Best were getting at Manchester United, but the Old Trafford crowd was twice the size of West Ham's, so Bobby thought the deal was fair.

Besides, the real money was to be made off the pitch. That had been obvious since 1962. Shortly after Bobby returned from the Chile World Cup, he was signed up on a two-year contract by a London-based agent called Bagenal Harvey, who specialized in clients from sport and the media and who was responsible for securing the Brylcreem poster of blessed memory. After that, the supply dried up, so Bobby bought his way out of the contract in favour of the services of West Ham's Jack Turner.

Jack's official job title at West Ham was Property Manager, although that hardly hinted at his actual role. He did everything from helping the apprentices with their income tax returns to acting as agony uncle and helping out with the scouting. In fact he had played a pivotal part in discovering Bobby – in 1955, acting on Ted Fenton's instructions, he had taken himself off to Flanders Field, East Ham, to watch him play for Leyton Boys in a schoolboy game. The otherwise favourable report he sent back to Ted Fenton contained the immortal words, 'Whilst he would not set the world alight . . .'

Jack was obviously no great prophet, but he made up for it later. It was on his advice that Bobby set up the sports good shop across the road from Upton Park. Very quickly, Bobby found he was making as much over the road as he was on the pitch, so Jack was someone whose judgement Bobby trusted.

One of the first spin-offs Jack negotiated for Bobby was a ghostwritten column with *Titbits*. That sounds as though it might be a top-shelf magazine but in fact it was a harmless tabloid weekly. Later on, Jack also organized columns in the football weekly, *Shoot*, and the *Daily Mirror* and got him some advertising work. One of them was made for television just after the 1966 World Cup and boasted the slogan, 'Call In At Your Local.' With Martin and Kathy Peters, Bobby and I had to sail into a pub and order drinks at a strangely under-populated bar. I laugh when I see it now. We all looked really uptight and self-conscious – not at all how you'd look if you really were in the pub with your friends.

Another commercial was for Bisto and had me preparing Bobby's favourite meal of calves' liver and bacon, then wrinkling up my nose at the end and saying, 'Ah, Bisto . . .'. Bobby didn't appear in that one. In fact, he didn't much like appearing in ads at all – he was quite shy. He accepted most things that came in, although there was the occasional offer

– usually drinks-based – which Jack Turner thought would be bad for his image. Bobby himself was resolute about not doing cigarette commercials. He was violently anti-smoking, but he had no such objections to Kelloggs Corn Flakes. In 1970 they paid him £3000 for a poster ad, which was serious money then.

One of the first things Bobby did with his new-found affluence was buy the Jaguar he had always longed for. We were also able to fulfill another long-held dream – a property abroad.

Not long after we moved to Manor Road, Bobby and one of his business partners, Freddie Harrison, got together to buy a house in Marbella. Pauline and Jimmy Tarbuck had a place there too, and so did Sean Connery. Sean was a real football fan and in fact he once babysat for us while we were on holiday. He said Dean and Roberta were among the best-behaved children he'd ever met. I was overcome with maternal pride.

While we were waiting for the house to be built, Bobby and I stayed with the children in the Marbella Club. That was owned by Prince Alphonso de Hohenloe, whose two sons, Prince Christophe and Prince Huberto, used to climb up trees to get to our rooms and play with Roberta and Dean. Olivia de Haviland, Laurence Harvey and Stewart Grainger were friends of the Prince, and we had dinner with them and other stars of that era. You would never catch me complaining about life in the fast lane, although with all those sumptuous meals we had to be careful it didn't become life in the fat lane.

We had some great times in Marbella over the years. A whole crowd of us had kids the same age. But forget any ideas of a blissfully relaxing few weeks spent lazing on a golden beach sipping sangria from a goblet with a royal crest on it. I'd get back to England more in need of a holiday than when we set out. Bobby's appetite for fun was inexhaustible. He was relentless.

His appetite for fun? And brandy and gin and tonic and crème de menthe, and the rest. Everybody used to drink in that era, before the health police got round to telling us it was a no-no, and sometimes we drank to extremes. Bobby didn't drink alcohol every day, but when he did he lost all his inhibitions. He went from being the repressed, uptight son of teetotal Doss and Bob, ever-conscious of what behove him as England captain, to a different Bobby, mischievous and irresponsible.

Holidaying among trusted friends, away from the gaze of press and public, allowed him to let rip as much as he wanted. Once it all got too much for me. We were at a party that went on until dawn began to break. I'd been through a succession of broken nights with Dean and had had enough of the partying for that night.

'Bobby, please, please let's go home now,' I begged him.

Instead, he turned to the waiter. 'Another gin and tonic, please.'

I was furious. 'If you want another one, well – here it is,' I said, and poured the contents of my glass over him.

That stopped him in his tracks. He looked at me and raised his arm, then licked it. 'Really, Teen,' he said with a lovely smile, 'you know I like it with a little less tonic.'

In contrast, the only time I ever saw Bobby completely incapacitated was in Marbella when we went out on a boat one day with a wealthy West Ham fan called Bill Larkin, known as 'Mr Peanuts' because that was his line of business. That summer he also had a new set of teeth, of which he was very proud, but at one point, while he was shouting at one of the kids, they flew out of his mouth and into the sea. Then they started bobbing away on the waves. Bobby dived in to retrieve them. I was scared – he'd had so much I was convinced he'd drown. But he found them and handed them back to Mr Peanuts before staggering back to shore and collapsing against the beach bar. He kept trying to prop himself upright but couldn't. He was slumped over a wall like a damp tea cloth.

Bobby was also quite vain. He might have been captain of England but there was still a lot of the East London Mod in his make-up. He liked a little bit of bling, too. Even so, he was never flash – no Essex Man medallions for him. The kind of jewellery he liked was his antique fob watch, an early present from me. Another favourite was the gold key chain I bought him from Aspreys, which he always kept hanging from one of his belt straps. On the end was a St Christopher, the size of a penny. The racing driver Graham Hill, father of Damon, was the only other person we ever saw with one like it. Bobby didn't wear a wedding ring – instead he had a bloodstone ring that I gave him when we got married.

The apogee of Bobby's dandy period was probably when *Tailor & Cutter* magazine listed him as one of the Ten Best Dressed Men of 1971, between the Duke of Windsor and Lord Snowdon. The citation read:

Ninth place goes to Mr Ice Cool himself, Bobby Moore, England and West Ham captain. His brand of elegance is based on two facts. His cool-as-a-cucumber personality does wonders for good clothes, but his stint as a model for Horne Brothers has gained him sartorial status. Bobby Moore has helped make the footballer part of the modern social scene.

Bobby actually fancied himself as a Steve McQueen lookalike, and as soon as he'd seen Steve in *The Thomas Crown Affair* he had two shirts made for himself exactly like the ones Steve wore – pink with maroon banding round the collar and cuffs, and pale blue trimmed with royal blue.

He also tried to grow his curly hair long, and he and his tall, buck-toothed business partner, Freddie Harrison, would head off to Covent Garden and hairdresser-of-the-month to have their coiffures blow-dried. Once the stylist was a bit over-enthusiastic and Bobby came home with a bouffant; we fell about laughing. I'm sure it was only co-incidence, but he ended his flirtation with long hair shortly afterwards.

I was fond of Freddie, but his business partnership with Bobby was really chapter after chapter of slightly comic disasters. Freddie was in the ladies' suede and leather-wear business and he encouraged Bobby and another friend in the rag trade, Morris Keston, to go into the suede and leatherwear market for men. Someone else who was involved was Jimmy Tarbuck and, knowing him to be an astute businessman, Bobby enthusiastically became a partner. The company started off with an East London factory and a showroom in Percy Street in the West End. Morris Keston pulled out soon after Harrison-Moore was launched, but the firm then expanded into a bigger factory in Essex and promptly ran into production problems because of a national power crisis that resulted in the government's infamous three-day working week.

They closed down the Essex factory and sub-contracted the work to outside manufacturers before Freddie Harrison had the idea of buying a small factory in Cyprus. Things had just got off the ground there when Turkey invaded the island. The factory was in the wrong place at the wrong time and they couldn't get the goods out.

Harrison-Moore wasn't the only venture that Bobby got involved in at around that time. A Hatton Garden jeweller persuaded him to establish Bobby Moore Jewellery. That completely failed to sparkle. Then, with a clothing retailer called David Walker, he set up Bobby Moore Shirts and Ties, a bespoke shirt-making business. Bobby arranged to have the goods made up in Manchester at a shirt-making company part-owned by Mike Summerbee. Mike, already a successful businessman, was part of the celebrated Manchester City side that included Francis Lee and Colin Bell. He was an affable man, sloping-shouldered and with a sensitive face that gave no hint to opponents of what lay in store for them on the pitch. In the Seventies, an era of some noted hard men, he was one of the hardest – George Best once said that when he tackled Mike, the only person he hurt was himself.

Mike and Bobby got on well – they often roomed together on England trips when, after experiencing Bobby's fastidiousness at first hand, Mike observed admiringly, 'Bobby's the only man who could have a bath and get out dry.' How did Bobby manage that? He would stand in the bath and flick the water off himself, towel one leg dry and only then step out – onto the dry leg. I was really impressed the first time I saw this routine. I had to copy it. Neither of us ever got a bathmat wet.

Customers for Bobby Moore shirts would be measured up in London and the orders sent up to Mike's factory in Manchester. Unfortunately the demand exceeded the supply and only a few were produced. Bobby might have kept the bathmat dry, but he got a soaking on those shirts.

But at that point Bobby's football career was so lucrative that he was able to take the setbacks in his stride. Life was good.

Other highlights from that time included an invitation to Downing Street for a reception held in honour of the heroes of the 1969 US moon landing, Buzz Aldrin, Neil Armstrong and Michael Collins. It's often been said that the feelgood factor from England's World Cup win in 1966 was what kept Harold Wilson's Labour in government in the General Election of that year. Nearly four years later, the World Cup in Mexico was almost certain to be followed by another election. England were strongly fancied to retain the Jules Rimet Cup and it's entirely possible that the Prime Minister was hoping that a little more of Bobby's stardust would rub off on him.

A lot of the top entertainers and sports stars of the day were there and a fantastic evening was rounded off by the specially composed ditty that Kenny Lynch sang to Harold Wilson, which began with the immortal words: 'Hey neighbour, Vote Labour . . .'.

Was Kenny a Labour supporter? I don't know, but he certainly was that night. After the reception some of us headed onwards to Trader Vic's at the Hilton. Our party included Lillian Board, the 400 metre runner who had won a silver medal at the 1968 Mexico Olympics and was crowned European champion the following year. She was a stunning, willowy blonde who, if she hadn't died so cruelly of cancer just after her twenty-second birthday at the end of 1970, would surely have gone on to even greater triumphs. As we went into the Hilton, Bobby and Jimmy Tarbuck held open the door for her. 'If you ran, could we chase you?' said Jimmy.

Bobby said, 'We'd never catch her up.'

Lillian's eyes danced as she said, 'I'd slow down for you, Mr Moore.'

I don't want to give the impression that the life Bobby and I led consisted of one continuous luxury holiday/high-life knees-up incorporating the odd visit to rub shoulders with the great and the good in Downing Street. Events like the ones I've described stay in the mind precisely because they were special, and we felt so lucky to be able to experience them. But our life in those days mainly centred around enjoying ourselves at home with friends, watching our children grow and sharing wonderful times as a family. Having that warmth and closeness helped us get through a period that for a while blotted out all the blessings that had been bestowed on us: my mother's death in 1968.

She hadn't been well and came to stay with us so we could keep an eye on her. One day we found her in a coma.

She had tests in hospital but nothing showed up on them and in any case she was so young – only 51 – that we couldn't believe anything was seriously wrong at first. But she was getting worse rather than better and one night, in the autumn of that year, she told me quite matter-of-factly that she had 'seen' Nanny Wilde, her mother, and she knew she was going to be with her soon.

She went into a coma again soon afterwards and was taken back to hospital. It was a brain tumour. Bobby and I slept together on a camp bed beside her and we were there when she took her last breath. Her final words to Bobby were 'Look after Tina,' and to me, 'I love you.'

I was devastated by her death, just inconsolable. At first I missed her so much I couldn't bear to part with her clothes. They stayed in the cupboards in the spare room at Manor Road where I'd stored them. The smell of her perfume was still on them, and if I opened the cupboard doors the air would fill with 'My Sin' by Arpege.

It's hard to put into words what a marvellous person she was without the phrases sounding hackneyed, but she was just the most vibrant, funny and giving woman and a terrific character. And Bobby loved her, he truly did. Even now, I think about her every day.

CHAPTER SEVEN

Green Fire, White Lace

The phone rang just after two in the morning and I heard a voice saying, 'Tina? Tina Moore?'

'Yes,' I mumbled sleepily.

It was a journalist from the press agency, Reuters. 'Have you heard what's happened to Bobby?' he said.

'What?' I was immediately wide awake. 'Is he OK? Has there been an accident?'

'No, no, no. He's been arrested for theft.'

'Oh my God. Tell me again. Slowly.'

'He's meant to have stolen a bracelet from the hotel gift shop in Bogota. Bobby Charlton shielded him so he could do it.'

'Oh, don't be ridiculous! You're having me on. Do you know what time of night it is over here? Then I unplugged the phone. It had to be a prank. I went straight back to sleep.

Around 5.30 I woke up again because I could hear the hum of voices. I looked outside. The whole of my front garden and most of the street was filled up with reporters, photographers and TV cameramen. The realization hit me. I thought, 'This is for real. Bobby is under arrest in Colombia on a trumped up charge of stealing a bracelet and in ten days the World Cup is due to start.'

It was the middle of May 1970. Tune into Radio One and you'd probably hear the strains of 'Back Home', an infuriatingly catchy football anthem sung by the 1970 England World Cup Squad. The first verse went like this:
'Back home
They'll be thinking about us
When we are far away.
Back home
They'll be really behind us
In every game we play.'
Little did the nation know that Bobby liked putting 'Back Home' on the record player whenever we came home with a crowd after partying. Then he would ride round and round the sofa on a child's bicycle. I would follow on a scooter while someone else would be leading a merry group of revellers all goose-stepping on the carpet in time to the beat.

In fact, I'd been wildly looking forward to travelling to Mexico to watch the World Cup. The location would be glamorous, the culture would be excitingly different and I was making the trip with three of the other England wives,

Judith Hurst, Kathy Peters and Frances Bonetti, who was married to the Chelsea and England reserve goalie, Peter. I had also been signed up by the *Daily Sketch* to produce a World Cup Diary with the help of their New York correspondent, Dermot Purgavie.

When the tournament was finished, Bobby and I planned to fly down to Acapulco with Geoff and Judith for a holiday. Judith and I had had a great time buying outfits for our amazing trip. We spent hours, and hundreds, at Tracey's in Bond Street, *the* place to shop. I had a white lace trouser suit, a blue catsuit with a low-slung hipster belt and flared bottoms, a pair of platform shoes, and an outfit that consisted of black linen pants, matching bandana and a black chiffon shirt with red and yellow embroidery. All I needed was a sombrero and I would have looked more Mexican than the Mexicans.

I'd even gone on a diet. I needn't have bothered. I was so frantic with worry over Bobby and that bracelet that I lost pounds without even trying. It was an emerald and diamond bracelet, or it would have been had it existed. It's one of the most famous pieces of invisible jewellery in modern history.

Did Bobby actually steal it? No way. It was the last thing Bobby would do, ever. He was the most honest, upright person you would ever hope to meet. But for some reason, the controversy has pursued him beyond the grave. Even now, when someone finds out who I was married to, the chances are that sooner or later I'll be asked what the real story is behind what happened in a gift shop called Green Fire at the Tequendama Hotel, Bogota, in Colombia in May 1970.

After I'd woken up to the buzz emanating from the media encampment, I got dressed and hurried downstairs to open the door.

'Is it true?' I called out to the reporters.

Yes, it seemed it was. I shut the door again to shouts of, 'Tina! Tina, can we have a word?'

At that point the phone rang again. It was Bobby, talking at about five hundred words a minute. He was frantic in case he got cut off. 'Tina, have you heard? Are you all right?'

'We're all fine. Don't worry about us. But Bobby – what on earth's happening?'

The phone line went dead. I rattled the receiver up and down for ages, to no effect.

I couldn't bear the idea of waiting around doing nothing. I phoned the FA, who put me on to the Home Office, who passed me on in their turn to the Foreign Office. 'Don't worry,' they said. 'Everything's being done to ensure Bobby's immediate release. He could be out any moment now.'

Next came a call from Morris Keston, a friend and great admirer of Bobby's despite his being a lifelong Spurs fan. 'Get yourself on the next flight to Bogota,' he said. 'I'll pay.'

'Thanks, Morris, that's a really kind offer,' I said, 'but they're saying Bobby's going to be released any minute. I don't want to arrive out there and find I've missed him altogether.'

I really did think it was all going to be over that quickly.

It was hard for me, thousands of miles away, to know what was happening. Most of the negotiations for Bobby's release were being carried on in private. The phone communications between England and Mexico were unreliable and expensive. A three-minute call cost a small fortune and letters could take up to a week to arrive.

Bobby had already been away for a couple of weeks when the incident happened. The England squad had flown out to Mexico to get used to playing at the high altitude. From there they went on to Colombia for the first of two friendlies.

They checked into the Tequendama hotel, where Bobby went into the Green Fire jewellery shop with Bobby Charlton. Bobby Charlton was thinking of buying something for Norma, his wife. They had a quick look around and checked some prices with the shop assistant but didn't ask her to get anything out of the display cabinets. Then they wandered out again to sit around the foyer with the other players.

After a while an older woman came out of the shop and asked them to go back in again. The two Bobbies weren't suspicious. They assumed the shop assistant had found something that Norma Charlton might like, so they followed her back in.

'Some jewellery is missing,' she said.

'Search us,' Bobby said immediately. 'We haven't touched anything.'

After that, everything happened very quickly. The police arrived and it was a very tense as they waved their guns around. The two Bobbies had to make a formal statement to the police. Both already suspected a set-up. What's more, with the team staying at the hotel another three days, both were worried that something might be planted in their rooms, so there was relief all round when the squad left Bogota to fly to Ecuador for another friendly. In the words of Kenneth Wolstenholme, they thought it was all over. It wasn't. On the way back to Mexico after the game, they had to change planes in Bogota. There was an arrest warrant waiting for Bobby.

Bobby thought he only had to go to the police station and confirm his original statement, but instead he was taken to a court house where the shop assistant identified him as the thief. While the rest of the team flew on to Mexico, he was put under house arrest. Instead of preparing to lead England into their first World Cup game, he found himself sharing a bedroom with two armed guards at the house of

Senor Alfonso Senior, the Director of the Colombian
Football Federation.

'It could be worse,' he thought. 'At least I'm not locked
in a cell.' That would have really affected him physically
and psychologically. As it was, it didn't do a lot for his
insomnia.

Back in Chigwell, that first day passed in a blur of con-
fusion and anxiety, but I made it as normal as I could so
as not to alarm the children. Dean was only a toddler, but
Roberta had just started school and I was worried about
the effect on her if one of the other children said something
to her. Kids can be cruel without thinking. So I asked her
headmistress to keep an eye on things and when Roberta
came home that afternoon, the only thing she had to
report was that one little girl said, 'Your daddy's found a
necklace.'

Doss took it very badly. It was understandable. Here was
her perfect son, the light of her life, and his name had been
besmirched. I wanted to check that she was coping all right
but it was a nightmare trying to get away because everywhere I went I was followed by a stampede of reporters.

The police came up with the idea of giving me a body
double. One of them brought round a dark wig for me and
I put that on while the au pair, adopting the traditional
disguise of blonde wig, big hat and sunglasses, drove off in
my car.

The press posse followed her, allowing me to slip out of the side door. I crawled to the bottom of the garden, then climbed over the back fence and ran to my neighbour's garage. Another policeman was waiting for me there in another car. He threw a blanket over me as I crouched in the back seat.

We sped off to Bobby's parents' house in Barking. Doss was waiting for us. She was still very upset, but managed to raise a wry chuckle when I sprinted from the car to the front door with the blanket over my head.

Reassuring each other made me forget my own anxieties and in fact while I was there, a call from Bobby came through. It was such a relief to know he was safe, even though the ice-cool front he'd been keeping up crumbled when he heard my voice. We both broke down. I didn't know what to say. Nor did he. But one thing was certain right from the start – his innocence. I didn't have to ask him if he'd taken the bracelet. It didn't occur to me. It just wasn't him.

The press hadn't moved from outside the house when I got back. I spent the next two days under virtual house arrest myself, reading the papers, watching television and trying to prise more information out of the Foreign Office. The lovely Dr Kennedy came round without being summoned and gave me some tranquillizers but I didn't get very much sleep.

117

I kept thinking, 'Mud sticks. Whatever happens, there are going to be people who won't believe Bobby is completely innocent.' I had visions of some sick soul daubing 'Thief' on our walls.

I felt as if I couldn't take any more. I went through the body double routine with the au pair again and smuggled the children out of the back of the house. I drove straight to Judith Hurst's.

'It just goes on and on,' I sobbed. 'I don't know what to do. They keep telling me Bobby's going to be released. And every time I look at the papers or turn on the TV, there's his picture.'

Judith didn't hesitate. She just took us in.

In Bogota, Bobby's ordeal continued. At ten in the morning on 27 May, he was taken back to Green Fire in the Tequendama Hotel, where the shop owner and assistant were waiting for him. Bobby had to take part in a re-enactment of the incident in front of a judge, plus the dozens of spectators with their faces pressed to the shop window and glass door.

As the tiny shop was crowded with legal personnel and the testimonies of the Green Fire people were ludicrously inconsistent, everything had a farcical quality. Bobby was sure he would be freed from custody then and there. Then he found out that a surprise witness had been brought in. The man was claiming that he had been walking past the

118

shop when he looked through the door and saw Bobby in the act of stealing the bracelet. A chill ran down Bobby's spine. 'I'm not out of trouble yet,' he thought. 'This bloke's a phoney. I know the truth, but how the hell am I going to prove it?'

After the re-enactment, the rest of the day was taken up by legal arguments in the judge's chambers in the court house. At the end, the judge still hadn't come to a decision.

Bobby was driven back to his room at the house of the Director of the Colombian Football Federation, Alfonso Senior.

He was certain he'd be released before the start of the World Cup, but he was worried about the shape he'd be in by then. He knew he had to have some sort of work-out. The next day, Alfonso Senior got permission for him to train on a public football pitch. The jungle drums had been beating and by the end, Bobby's work-out had turned into a kick-about friendly with a bunch of barefoot local kids in front of a media posse.

After that came another appearance before the judge. This one only lasted ten minutes. Finally, the judge ruled that he had heard nothing so far that could incriminate Bobby. Bobby was freed on condition that he signed a declaration that he would make himself available for further questioning at a Colombian consulate in Mexico or London if necessary.

Bobby had no problem with signing. He had nothing to

hide. On 29 May he was finally on his way to Guadalajara. The airport at Bogota was packed with thousands of Colombians, cheering and jostling to catch his eye and touch him. By now most of Colombia had realized he was the innocent victim of a notorious extortion racket that targeted visiting celebrities. They gave him the full-on national hero treatment.

Bobby's flight had to make an overnight stop in Mexico City. There, accommodation had been arranged for him at the home of the British Embassy's Information Officer. The night quickly took on a farcical aspect. Bobby hadn't been there long when an immensely tall man in a loud check jacket and green trousers walked in via the back door. Lou Wade was indulging in his usual hobby of following Bobby all over the world and had managed to track him down. The location was meant to be a secret. Obviously no one had made that clear to the world's reporters and cameramen. They were all crowded around the front of the house under the full glare of television arc lights.

The housekeeper was still trying to come to terms with Lou's flamingo-like presence when someone else appeared. Jimmy Greaves, Bobby's former England team-mate, had got himself to the Information Officer's house the long way round, by souped-up Ford Escort. With Roger Clark, a top driver of the time, he had taken part in the World Cup Rally, a race from London to Mexico. He had followed Lou over a wall at the back of the house.

'Fancy a lager?' he said to Bobby.

The housekeeper rounded on him. 'Who are you? No one unauthorized is allowed in.'

'Please, I can vouch for him,' said Bobby. 'He's a great friend of mine and we've played together for many years.'

'Sorry. He must leave.'

Jimmy left via the way he came. Two minutes later the front doorbell rang and when the housekeeper went to answer it, Jimmy was standing there, his sunny, impish face creased with laughter.

'Is it possible to see Mr Moore?'

'Who shall I say it is?'

'I'm Jimmy Greaves, an old friend of his.'

'Please come in, he will be very glad to see you.'

It was, Bobby said to me later, 'typical Jimmy'.

The girls and I were heading for Guadalajara too, at last. By then I'd been assured that Bobby was all right but even so, I couldn't wait to get there to see him and make sure for myself.

From the moment we boarded the plane at Heathrow, the cabin was buzzing with excitement. A huge number of fans were travelling out to Mexico and one by one they were coming up to me, telling me Bobby would be all right. Every single one was full of indignation about what had happened and all my fears about people actually believing Bobby had done something wrong disappeared.

Besides, deep down I knew Bobby would cope. He had conquered cancer. He was a winner and he always rose to the occasion. He would show people that nothing would stop him playing his heart out for England. For the first time, I relaxed and allowed the excitement of the trip to wash over me.

I did experience one more scary moment. That was as I went to step off the plane, only to find myself surrounded by armed guards. My heart was in my mouth. 'What's happening?' I said. But it was just to give me a hassle-free passage through customs before rushing me to the hotel.

Alf had made an exception to his no-contact-with-wives rule. Bobby and I were allowed an hour alone together. Judith Hurst and I were sharing a room, but tactfully she made herself scarce. I ran to him and fell into his arms, in floods of tears. He just couldn't stop kissing me and hugging me.

'Are you really all right?' I said eventually.

'Yeah. A-OK. Ready for anything.'

I just looked at him in awe. He'd been falsely accused, isolated from his team and left on his own in a foreign country, yet here he was, coolly and calmly focused on bringing the World Cup back to England. I could only think once again: *what a man.*

By the time the tournament started, it was as if Bobby's ordeal had never happened. The girls and I all went to watch England's first game, against Rumania. I was actually quite tense and felt a bit superstitious. I'd worn the same dress to every match in 1966 because I didn't dare put anything else on in case it changed our luck. This time I settled for the white lace trouser suit.

We kept seeing familiar faces in the crowd – Ron Greenwood, Don Revie, Joe Mercer, Dave Sexton, Bertie Mee. It was a little corner of England, and the fans looked great with their top hats, rosettes, flags and red-white-and-blue umbrellas. We were wrapped patriotically in a huge Union Jack to keep the rain off when Geoff Hurst scored the winner. We had a wonderful view of it – it was the first time I had ever sat behind the posts – and we all went mad.

It was going to be the white lace trouser suit until further notice.

From My World Cup Diary. *Daily Sketch*, June 4 1970:
WHY I THINK ALF'S RIGHT TO KEEP THE SEXES APART
After the great game against Rumania, Sir Alf Ramsey relaxed his rules on segregation in separate hotels and allowed our husbands to see us.

They had to be back by eleven, though.

Certainly Alf is strict, but I think it's essential that he should be. This is a serious business and not a joy ride for the team.

I don't think it would affect Bobby if I was around –

nothing distracts his attention from the game – but I still agree with the rules.

They have nothing to do, as many people seem to believe, with keeping the players celibate. I don't believe it. If that theory is true, why haven't the Vatican won the World Cup? Bobby and I never consider sex in relation to football.

My World Cup Diary was trailed as 'An Insider's View'. That was ironic since at one stage the closest we got to the boys was to borrow a pair of binoculars to watch them sitting on the opposite side of the stadium at Brazil v Czechoslovakia.

Bobby called me every day from the team hotel, but usually we got cut off in mid-conversation. In those days, everyone complained about the British telephone system but it was a futuristic marvel compared to Mexico's. The only time it seemed to work properly was between two and six in the morning. Dermot Purgavie, the *Daily Sketch* New York correspondent who was putting together my thoughts for the column, was based in Guadalajara but in another hotel. The only time I could do my piece with him was between those hours, which was all right when the girls and I had been out after a match but not so good when I had to get up to do it.

My World Cup column wasn't the place to disclose that the boys would occasionally sneak out and find their way to our hotel. It would have been Alf's worst nightmare. We had to be especially careful because Vicky, Lady Ramsey, was also staying there. We had flown out on the same plane, but she was in first class while we were in standard and we certainly wouldn't have dared to join her. She was a lovely person, in fact, but we viewed her with awe and gave her a wide berth.

By the time we'd been in Mexico a few days, the girls and I had already practically worn ourselves out laughing. Kathy Peters was a real scream – literally, in one instance, when a giant rat rushed past her in the street. But it was a beautiful location, Bobby was safe and yes, Alf let us join our husbands at one cocktail party.

I surpassed myself when I got talking to one of my fellow guests, a really good-looking young blond guy.

'What do you do?' I said. 'Are you with TV?'

He looked slightly surprised and said, 'Well, no. I'm playing for England.'

Bobby suddenly loomed at my side. 'Tina, this is Colin Bell. Sorry, Col. Tina Moore, you are going home.'

That didn't find its way into my *Daily Sketch* column, either.

There was a strong Brazilian contingent staying at our hotel, along with the English fans and some of the British press. They were incredibly friendly despite our national rivalry – we were due to meet Brazil in the second game of Group Three. We could even match entertainer with entertainer. Amongst the Brazilians was the singer Wilson Simonal, Brazil's answer to Tom Jones, while England could offer Kenny Lynch.

Also with the Brazilians was a lovely man called Helio, a great friend of Pele's. Bobby and I had met him on previous trips to Brazil and much to my delight he invited a group of fans, including me, to visit the Brazil training camp. I was in a quandary about whether to go or not. I didn't want it to be seen as consorting with the enemy on the eve of their greatest battle. But when I mentioned it to Bobby during our next phone call he encouraged me to take up the Brazilians' invitation. 'You might even try and find out what their strategy and tactics are going to be,' he laughed.

Pele was practically the first person we saw there. He was just wonderful, a nice, polite, respectful man with lovely kind eyes. He told me how much he admired Bobby, and I couldn't believe that someone so revered all over the world could also be so unassuming.

'Right, Tina,' said another of the Brazil players. 'We're going to win the World Cup, but we'll give it to you to put on your mantelpiece.'

What a cheek!

I'd always been able to follow a football game reasonably well, although when I went to matches I mostly just watched Bobby and I could never claim to be an expert on any finer points of the game beyond those exhibited by a certain West Ham Number Six.

What I hadn't expected when I went to Mexico was how much I would enjoy the football itself. It had something to do with the intense and passionate way it was played by the Latino countries and it struck a chord within me. Years later, I was to get the same vibes from an Argentinian dance when a friend introduced me to the tango.

England's second game in Group Three was a case in point. It was the most absorbing, charged and tense game of football I had ever been to. Though, as you might say, shame about the result. 1–0 to Brazil. Afterwards I just felt emotionally and physically drained. Kathy Peters even cried.

In spite of the score, it was the best game I had ever seen Bobby play – Pele was so swept away that he kissed him afterwards and the two of them swapped shirts. That made two in the Moore household, because I was given a shirt when we went to the Brazil training camp.

I did think a draw would have been fairer, and we were all convinced that we would meet Brazil again in the Final, and win.

As for the Mexican supporters, I had never seen anything like the hysteria. It was less like a football match than a gladiatorial contest, with the crowd providing the tribal war dances accompanied by the bands they had brought along.

There was a lot of hostility towards England. Latin

America hadn't forgotten the way Alf Ramsey described the Argentine team as 'animals' in 1966 after the infamous quarter-final at Wembley when Argentina played dirty and Antonio Rattin, ordered off, provoked a rebellion by refusing to go. Four years later, England's popularity hardly soared when it was announced that they were bringing out all their own supplies from home, from baked beans to a team bus. Mexico took it personally.

The Mexicans in Guadalajara had adopted Brazil, the only Latino team in Group Three, and decided to help them through to the next stage of the tournament by besieging the England team hotel. For hours on end they stood outside, blocking traffic, chanting, beating drums, blowing bugles, waving banners, breaking bottles and driving by in continuous convoy, blasting their horns. The police looked on and shrugged. It was like the aftermath of a revolution.

The most diabolical thing during the game was when the Brazil supporters released a pigeon with yellow and green streamers tied to its legs. The poor thing flew round and round the stadium, trying to avoid all the people trying to grab it as a trophy, until eventually it flopped exhausted on the pitch.

And the white lace trouser suit had to go, of course. A major decision had to be made. Was it to be the Mexican ensemble? I thought not. It was on with the blue catsuit – with platform shoes to give myself, and England, a lift.

*   *   *

It worked for England's final game in Group Three. We beat Czechoslovakia 1–0 to finish second behind Brazil. That meant the boys faced a 200-mile coach ride to Leon for their quarter-final match against West Germany.

We four girls stayed in Guadalajara to watch the match on TV. Gordon Banks had had to drop out with food poisoning but England's loss was Frances Bonetti's gain – her Peter was drafted into goal, so she could cheer on her man at last.

It was Peter 'The Cat' Bonetti's first game in a World Cup and he only learnt he was in the side less than three hours before kick-off. Gordon Banks was a legend and even though England had lost to Brazil in the second match, one save he had made from Pele made us feel we were invincible. On the other hand, Peter was one of the best goalies in the tournament. Frances was nervous for him but like the rest of us, she totally believed in her man.

We were jubilant at first and the margaritas were flowing as England built up a 2–0 lead through Alan Mullery and Martin Peters, but it finished up as the most sickening and disappointing game I had ever watched.

There were twenty minutes to go and we were counting down to the final whistle when Franz Beckenbauer, England's old foe from the '66 World Cup, scored for West Germany. It seemed such a fluke, as if he had tried a shot more as something to do at the end of a run rather than having a real crack at goal. We just expected Peter to fall on it smartly, but he dived in a slow-motion arc over the ball and let it travel into the net. The Cat wasn't looking like The Cat at all.

Just after that, Alf put Colin Bell on in place of Bobby Charlton, and ten minutes later Martin Peters was going off to make room for Norman Hunter. After only a few seconds, West Germany made it 2–2 with another fluke, a back-header from Uwe Seeler. It was hardly Peter's fault. It just looped over his head and under the bar. We were flabbergasted. 2–0 up and coasting, and now the match was going into extra time. It couldn't be happening.

Extra time was a nightmare. Gerd Muller, who hadn't done anything for most of the game, volleyed home the winner. At the end all four of us dissolved into tears. We just couldn't help it. The men had fought so hard, and now the work and hopes of four years had been destroyed, through two fluke goals. Little did Frances realize that for ever and all time people were going to be pointing the finger at her Peter as the man responsible for losing England the World Cup, when really he had just been so unlucky. It was a huge task that Peter had taken on, coming into the cauldron of Leon at only three hours notice to play his first ever game in the World Cup. The Cat had had no chance to find his feet – or his paws.

Bobby rang that night. Not being an emotional person, he didn't say much about how he felt, but he sounded very flat and low. It really was the worst time to be a footballer's wife. What on earth could we say to our men?

The team was absolutely broken up about it. Everyone had been showering compliments on Bobby for the way he played, but as far as he was concerned, that was of no consequence – England had lost. He really, really felt it. Before they set off for Mexico he'd been convinced they had a huge chance of retaining the World Cup. He was much more confident than he'd been at a similar stage in 1966. He could see how full the lads were of fire and energy.

Even though he'd just played so stupendously, it was one of those times when he did wonder if he could have done more. But other than grabbing the jersey from Peter Bonetti and saving all those goals himself, what more was there to do?

He said that when he got back to the hotel with the rest of the team, they found Gordon Banks still glued to the match on TV. There had been a delay in transmission because of some technical problems, and Gordon thought he was watching the game live. Even when it was over, he still assumed England had won because they were 2–0 up on the TV.

'We got beat,' Bobby told him.

'You're having me on,' said Gordon.

Then he spotted Bobby Charlton behind him. The man was in tears.

*   *   *

131

There was one funny aspect. The girls and I didn't know whether the boys were coming to join us in Guadalajara or heading straight for Acapulco, our holiday destination. Just as Bobby said, 'We're going – ' the phone cut out. In the end we made an educated guess, packed and left for Acapulco. Meanwhile, the boys went to Guadalajara. Not only had they lost the World Cup but they had lost their wives as well.

Once we were all reunited in Acapulco, life was fun again. We went to the Villa Vera Racquet Club, set on a hilltop, where each *cabana* featured a pool half indoors and half outside. It was a small, extremely chic hotel and the most sumptuous I had ever stayed in. Bobby and I loved it. The privacy meant we could really relax and enjoy the beauty of Acapulco. We drank exotic drinks on the beach while wearing flower garlands – even Bobby.

Bobby was never required to return to Colombia and make himself available for questioning. He was determined to see that the incident was properly closed, though. He wanted his name completely cleared. Through a solicitor in England, we hired a Colombian barrister to sift through the evidence and prepare a report. It revealed that the Colombian police had found out that just after the incident the shop owner had met up with the witness who claimed to have watched Bobby take the bracelet from outside the shop. The witness turned out to be a shady character in the gem trade. The shop owner offered him money to testify and the witness agreed, thinking it would put him in the shop owner's good books. They got together to cook up a story.

Even though there was so obviously a plot to frame Bobby, and it was widely known all the way to the top of the Special Branch of the Colombian police, it wasn't until 1975 that Bobby heard from the Foreign Office that the case was in effect closed.

Even now, the story refuses to go away. On the eve of the 2002 World Cup, a programme about Bobby was shown on television. It drew heavily on Bobby's biography, updated after his death in 1993 to reflect what had taken place since its first publication in 1976. In at least one way, these books are distinctly different, in spite of having the same author. In the earlier, authorized version, it's maintained that there was no bracelet. In the updated edition, it says that one night, while 'mellowed' by a few drinks, Bobby hinted that one of the younger England players might have taken it for a prank.

In fact, that piece of gossip has gone the rounds for years. I had the story repeated to me once again only the other day. I really wish it hadn't been given currency in the updated biography, with Bobby no longer here to confirm or deny the latest version. The story certainly wasn't what Bobby told me and, as the author wrote in the first version of the book, at the time the bracelet affair took place,

Bobby had only one true friend and confidante – me. Bobby was quoted as saying that although some of his friends would be upset to hear it, I truly was the only one he trusted because I wasn't interested in him as a footballer but in HIM as someone I loved and cared for.

Yes, Bobby was a private man, a very complicated man, and he had the ability to keep things to himself. But I am positive that he would have disclosed that to me, as he did the rest of his innermost thoughts and feelings at the time. He never mentioned it.

That doesn't mean there was no bracelet at all. There was one. While we were in Acapulco I gave him a gold identity bracelet as a keepsake of the Bogota affair. But it was bought, not stolen.

CHAPTER EIGHT

Naughty Boy

I didn't realize at the time, but that defeat against West Germany in Leon was the end of an era. When the 1970–71 season started, Bobby was one of only five Boys of '66 left in the England team. Ray Wilson, George Cohen and Roger Hunt had already stepped down and when the team returned from Mexico, the two Charlton brothers and Nobby Stiles retired, too. It was sad.

By that time West Ham's Big Three were down to two as well. In March 1970, Martin Peters had gone to Spurs in a part-exchange deal which brought Jimmy Greaves to Upton Park. Bobby and Jimmy went way back. Jimmy was an East Ham boy and during the 1966 World Cup they had roomed together. Jimmy had been the main England striker until he got injured and Geoff Hurst became his permanent replacement. Bobby found him packing his bags on the morning of the Final after Alf had broken the news to him. He had to console him, and Jimmy never really got over his disappointment at missing out.

He was the kind of player who was invisible for a lot of a game then seemed to pop up through a trap door to score a brilliant goal before disappearing again. He always ran with his head poked forward and his face wore an intense expression that broke rapidly into a huge grin. When he arrived at West Ham in the spring of 1970, Bobby was delighted. It wasn't just that Jimmy was a sunny, smiling character. He scored twice on his West Ham debut against Manchester City and got four more in the six games that followed. He had really lifted the team and Bobby was looking forward to what they might achieve during the 1970–71 season.

The answer was, not a lot. Jimmy's supply of goals dwindled very quickly. It wasn't known at the time but, although he conquered it later and went on to be a much-loved performer on TV, he was already battling with a drink problem. By the end of 1970, West Ham had slumped to twentieth in the table and relegation was an uncomfortable possibility. They needed a successful Cup run to turn things around. Instead they had what came to be known as the Blackpool Nightclub Affair, and Bobby was right in the centre of it.

I heard Bobby muttering on the phone to someone. After a while he put the receiver back and walked into the lounge. I looked at him expectantly. 'Who was that?'

'Stag.' That was his nickname for Brian Dear, a West

Ham team mate. Stone-faced, he made himself a drink. Then he said, 'Listen, Percy. There'll be something in the papers tomorrow and you're not going to like it.'

'What about?'

'Something that happened in Blackpool at the weekend. It isn't true, but you're still not going to like it.'

He was right. I didn't.

Over the next few hours and days, the story gradually unravelled. The previous Saturday the third round of the 1970–71 FA Cup had taken place. West Ham were drawn against fellow First Division strugglers Blackpool. The day before, New Year's Day, the team travelled to Lancashire by train in a cold snap that threatened to ice up every pitch north of Watford.

With the match already seemingly doomed to cancellation, Bobby and the rest of the squad faced a long evening kicking their heels in the Imperial Hotel. After dinner, Bobby decided to kill time in the foyer with the help of Jimmy, Brian Dear, Clyde Best and a round or two of lagers.

Bobby told me they were joined by a couple of members of the TV crew who were in Blackpool to film the match. Around 11 o'clock, the crew announced they were going on to the 007 Club, a Blackpool night spot owned by the former heavyweight boxer, Brian London. Bobby and the other three decided to go too. Bobby was adamant that all they did was spend an hour or so decorously sipping lager, apart from Clyde Best, who abstained altogether. It wasn't even 1 o'clock by the time they returned to the hotel.

Unfortunately, news leaked out of the escapade and even more unfortunately, the match did go ahead the next day and Blackpool beat West Ham 4–0. Bobby and Jimmy Greaves were the only two who played; Brian Dear was on the sub's bench and Clyde Best wasn't even picked. It seemed to be one of those typical West Ham performances in which just when they should have pulled out all the stops they lost humiliatingly.

Ron Greenwood, already dismayed by the result, was then confronted at Upton Park two days later by an outraged fan who said he had heard the team had been out clubbing. That made a bad situation worse, especially as the confrontation took place in front of the chairman, Reg Pratt.

It didn't stop there. The fan went to the papers with the story. There was a flurry of phone calls between Fleet Street, Brian Dear and Ron Greenwood, and eventually Brian 'fessed up to Ron and then called Bobby to warn him. That was when Bobby realized he had to come clean with me.

'And that's it?' I said.

'No. The papers have come up with this story about girls being involved. It isn't true, but they've got some phoney quotes from the hall porter saying we came in at three in the morning with them and started ordering champagne.'

Naughty Boy

The sparks flew between us, even though I didn't believe for one moment the stuff about the girls. That was just standard tabloid invention and I shouldn't have let it get to me. But I hated the thought that people would believe the lies that had been printed, and it was horrible and un-dignified to have the press camped outside the house again, so soon after Bogota.

With Roberta in tow, I was due to go on a ski-ing holiday with six of my Chigwell girlfriends – collectively we were known as the Magnificent Seven. The day after the news broke, we set off for the airport in a couple of hired cars. This soon turned into a convoy as reporters chased us to Heathrow. I kept my head down and tried to shield Roberta from the photographers, but a couple of the Seven thought it was the most Magnificent thing that had ever happened. They were beaming and posing for the cameras as if it were a fashion shoot.

The press loved it, of course. For them, it was a great story – Bobby Moore, captain of England and West Ham, caught having a night on the tiles twelve hours before a Cup tie that ended in woeful defeat. Bobby knew he'd behaved like an idiot, too. While I headed off with the Magnificent Seven, he drove over to West Ham to apologize to Ron and put him right about some of the more fantastic claims in the papers.

He needn't have bothered. Ron was just furious. 'I don't want to discuss it,' he said.

'But I want to tell you what really happened.'

'The matter will be dealt with by the board in due course.'

And that was that. Bobby was given a two-week suspension and fined a week's wages – £100. Although that in itself wasn't a heavy punishment, Bobby's relationship with Ron was already strained and the Blackpool incident damaged it beyond repair.

It was great to get away on that skiing jaunt, not just because I hated the stuff in the papers. I had a secret.

For some time, plans had been afoot for the BBC to make Bobby the subject of *This Is Your Life*. While the West Ham board were having crisis meetings about Blackpool, the BBC were having crisis meetings about Bobby. The fact that he was being branded all over the media as a naughty boy, and that everyone was smacking him left, right and centre, posed them a dilemma. Should they go ahead and show the programme or postpone it until the fingers had stopped wagging? Bobby, of course, was completely oblivious to this extra thickening of the brew. The whole point of *This Is Your Life* was that the subject had to be unaware of what was going on until the moment Eamonn Andrews surprised them with his Big Red Book.

Weeks before the Blackpool furore hit the papers, researchers had come along to Chigwell while Bobby was away for secret discussions about who they should have on the show. They were very nice boys, my age. We'd had a bottle of wine, and then another bottle of wine, then brandies, then liqueurs. Leaving behind me a lounge full of overflowing ashtrays and glasses of different shapes and sizes, I staggered up to bed around four in the morning. The next thing I knew was the sound of a key in the front door. Bobby was home a day earlier than I'd expected.

In he walked, to be greeted by a Bacchanalian scene, complete with record still going round and round on the turntable. Upstairs was a half-sloshed wife whose hastily concocted story was a mass of holes and contradictions. He accused me of having an affair and it wasn't until Eamonn Andrews popped up with his Big Red Book weeks later that the penny dropped and my reputation was saved.

I still have a tape of Bobby's appearance on the show and it makes wonderful, if unintentionally hilarious, viewing. It was The Show Of The Stiffs. I adopted a would-be elegant pose from which I didn't move all night. It wasn't only my hair that was set – it was as though all of me was lacquered. I never once uncrossed my legs and, of course, having been stuck in the same position all the way through recording, I was crippled with cramp when finally we were allowed to get up. I also got the giggles because Doss spoke her lines in such an extraordinary, fake posh accent: 'Ay always knew Robairt was keen on footbahll.'

But Bobby really put himself over well. That was great for him. Normally he found it hard to be natural on TV because he was quite shy and self-conscious and he would come over as a bit uptight.

Alfonso Senior, with whom he'd stayed while under house arrest in Bogota, had been flown over to appear on the show, as well as the two Jimmies, Greaves and Tarbuck. There was also a lady from the Thalidomide Trust, for which Bobby had done a lot of work on the quiet. The BBC showed a film clip of him playing with a boy born without limbs and Bobby was – well, just Bobby with him, natural and nice. He saw the boy, not the disability, and opened up to him whereas normally he was guarded. There was a brilliant exchange of dialogue between the two of them. 'Who do you support?' Bobby asked the boy.

'West Ham,' said the boy, adding with a cheeky smile, 'Who do you support?'

Bobby gave him a friendly cuff around the ear. 'Who do you think I support? Tina, Roberta and Dean, of course.'

Blackpool was forgotten. He was the nation's hero again.

Goodness knows what I didn't hear about in the matter of escapades like the one in Blackpool. Bobby tended to spare me the more florid details of any Boys' Night Out. It was only many years later that I discovered from Harry Redknapp that one night when they were away to Stoke, the team played so badly that Ron Greenwood said, 'No one goes out tonight. You're all confined to the hotel.' So some of them sneaked out through a window at the back of the hotel, ran across the motorway and found a cab to take them to a club. When they were sneaking back at four in the morning, Bobby slipped as he climbed over a fence and gashed his leg. The boys carried him back to the hotel where Rob Jenkins, the physio, secretly patched him up. On the train home the next morning he was limping, so they had to keep him out of Ron's sight.

The point about Bobby was that he loved a drink and he liked being one of the lads. He enjoyed being in the company of other men. In contrast, I never heard anything about his being a womanizer, even though the opportunities for him to stray were endless. It takes a special kind of man to be a world-renowned celebrity and have gorgeous women throwing themselves at him and still be able to resist, but that was him. He didn't need to boost his ego that way.

Right from the start of his fame, when he was photo-graphed surrounded by beautiful dolly-bird models in *Vogue* in 1962, it was obvious how attractive he was to women. I don't know how he managed it, but as he got more polished and sophisticated his looks got even better. Not that it was something I ever had to worry about. When it came to other women, he just had a blind spot.

The journalist Nigel Clarke, who helped Bobby produce his *Daily Mirror* columns and who was someone Bobby trusted completely professionally, once told me that Bobby was one of the only men he knew who could say 'No' to a gorgeous woman. I knew that already. That was why I was able to dismiss the stories about the girls at the hotel for the rubbish they were. I was completely confident in Bobby, and in my marriage.

Even so, I never thought the Blackpool episode showed Bobby at his best. One aspect that actually quite upset me was that he had allowed Clyde Best to be involved in it. Bobby had always been so aware of his responsibilities as captain. Jimmy and Brian were like Bobby – they could take it. But Clyde was a comparative baby. I knew Bobby made a point of including younger players when the lads were going drinking, to make them feel part of the set up, but this time he obviously didn't think through the possible consequences.

Maybe he just didn't care by then. Bobby had nothing left to prove at West Ham and desperately needed a new challenge. Perhaps what he did at Blackpool should have been interpreted as a cry for help. He and Ron Greenwood no longer connected and while Bobby admired him as a coach, he had lost respect for the man. Deep down, too, he suspected Ron no longer cared for or respected him very much either. I think he felt hurt.

CHAPTER NINE

A Long Way From Christchurch Road

West Ham fans of a certain age will remember the 1971–72 season mainly for one thing. It isn't for West Ham's continuing inconsistencies in the League. Neither is it for their FA Cup run, which ended when Huddersfield knocked them out in the fifth round. But even now they can recall the night Bobby had to play in goal.

By the time West Ham were drawn to play Stoke in the semi-final of the League Cup – forerunner of the Carling Cup – they had already knocked out Leeds, Liverpool and Sheffield United and were optimistic they could reach Wembley. Victory would bring them their first trophy since the European Cup Winners Cup in 1965.

The first leg was at the Victoria Ground early in December 1971 and they beat Stoke 2–1. Clyde Best scored the winner and the match also featured a genuine novelty. Bobby's tackling was so accurate and he had such control over his temper that he very, very rarely had his name taken, but this time was an exception. He was booked for a foul on Jimmy Greenhoff.

A week later, Stoke travelled down to Upton Park for the return leg and won 1–0 after Gordon Banks saved a penalty from Geoff Hurst. That meant a third game. Early on in the new year, West Ham and Stoke met again, at Sheffield Wednesday's ground, Hillsborough. The result was a 0–0 draw.

Nearly two months after this epic began, on 26 January 1972, a fourth match kicked off at Old Trafford. Quite early in the game, Bobby Ferguson, West Ham's goalie, collided with Terry Conroy and had to be taken off for treatment. That left an empty space between the goalposts, as the five substitutes rule hadn't yet been introduced. The only player willing to go in goal was Bobby, so he put on the gloves. Soon after that, Stoke were awarded a penalty. Bobby even got his hands to the initial shot from Mike Bernard. Sadly, he couldn't hold on to it and Mike scored from the rebound.

After that, Bobby Ferguson returned and Stoke won 3–2 in the end, but the children and I were so proud. We bought all the papers the next day for the children to add to their scrap books.

Although Bobby and I didn't know it at the time, 1972 proved to be a turning point in our lives. It was the year we moved from Manor Road to the house of our dreams.

A Long Way From Christchurch Road

I had been property-hunting with increasing seriousness for a year. I'd found both our previous places on my own and had Bobby's *carte blanche* to make the choice on his behalf. One of the places I looked at early on was a lovely Queen Mary house set in its own grounds. The vendor had actually pushed a letter through our door saying he had just the house for the captain of England to live in.

Judith Hurst came with me to look round it. Although the house itself was wonderful, it was too close to a busy road and by the time I stepped through the front door I had already decided to turn it down. Unfortunately, I didn't get the chance to issue the *coup de grâce* before being presented with a glass of the vendor's home-made elderberry wine.

'This is revolting,' I whispered to Judith.

She nodded, screwing up her face. 'But he's ever so proud of it. We can't hurt his feelings.'

I spotted a conveniently-placed crystal vase of flowers. Together, Judith and I edged towards it, then poured in the wine.

The water immediately turned dark red. So did our faces. We weren't a long time leaving after that.

The search for a new house continued, fruitlessly for a while. Then I heard of a building plot up for sale. 'It's in Stradbroke Drive,' said the estate agent. 'One of the two best roads in Chigwell.'

I didn't need to be told that. Stradbroke Drive was

etched in my childhood memories. One late summer long ago, I'd gone on the bus to Chigwell Row with Auntie Mum and Jenny to go blackberrying in Hainault Forest. We'd walked along Stradbroke Drive and I'd been awestruck by the lovely houses. It seemed impossible to believe that I would find myself living there, twenty-five years on. I really had to fight to get that parcel of land. For weeks I existed in a strange new world of bidding and counterbidding. The more I was thwarted, the more determined I was to get it, and finally the plot was ours.

Having a house designed and built from scratch was a giant project but I discovered I was in my element. We chose everything, from the bricks to the grouting. It was based on a lovely Georgian-style house owned by some friends of ours in nearby Abridge. Its best feature, a novelty in those days, was an extended porch raised on pillars. You could sweep up the drive and park the car underneath if it was raining. That suited the immaculate Bobby and the vain Tina down to the ground – no windswept look for us.

On either side of the panelled double front door were arched niches, one with a male head in bronze, the other a female one. Some wag usually stuck a cigarette in their mouths – very smart. Inside, a staircase swept down from a minstrels' gallery, like something out of *Gone With The Wind*.

One of the most challenging tasks of all was deciding

what to call the house. We experimented with various com-
binations of our Christian names, starting with Roedean
and then getting sillier and funnier until we ended up with
Beantrobe, Robotide, Ribena and Dire Boot. In the end we
settled for Morlands – the Land of the Moores. Original
or what?

Some of the work was still going on when we moved in.
One of Bobby's mates, the actor and singer Kenny Lynch,
owned a tile company. We commissioned Kenny's company to lay the kitchen floor for us and one of his tilers was
working in the house on his own when there was a knock
on the front door. He opened up to find a man in a boiler
suit, who said, 'I've come about the TV. Mr Moore rang
this morning to say you're getting poor reception. We're
going to have to take it away for repair.'

Kenny Lynch's tiler helped him carry the TV out to the
van, then went back to work. Van, man and TV were never
seen again.

But how we loved that house. It was everything we
wanted. Bobby's favourite room was his bar, hand-built
and decorated in brown and cream, with a shelf for all his
medals and cups. Considering the display included a gold
trophy for the Player of Players from the World Cup and
silver plates from the FA and FIFA, I'm amazed they never
went the way of the TV.

In fact, we did suffer a break-in once, but the burglar
was obviously a football fan. When he realized what he

had stolen and from whom, he must have been overcome with remorse. In fact, on the night of the burglary we had come home late and gone straight to bed without noticing anything missing. The next morning, Bobby opened the front door to go into work and found medals, cups and other treasures piled on the doormat. On top was a note that simply said, 'Sorry, Bob.'

Morlands boasted six bedrooms; ours had an en suite bathroom, complete with a round bath that was a nightmare to clean – but what the hell, we had someone to do that in those days. There were two more bathrooms and a shower room – it was a million miles from the tin bath that hung on a hook in Christchurch Road. Rodney Marsh used to go round looking for holes in the grouting and stick fivers inside for the children to find on treasure hunts.

The house had a very peaceful feeling; it was light and airy. It was arranged so that the French doors from the hall and drawing room opened onto a terrace (with fish pond, of course). The terrace was perfect for all the parties we had. We started the way we intended to go on, with a house-warming that went on well into the night and was a rip-roaring affair to rival Dean's christening bash. Once again, the policeman sent to investigate the noise was enticed indoors and presently he was sighted doing a very energetic twist.

Soon after we moved in, we were invited to dinner by the

next door neighbours, an old, very county Chigwell family. The wife was Cordon Bleu-trained and the food was sumptuous. When the time came to reciprocate the invitation, Bobby popped his head over the wall and asked them if they wanted to drop in for supper that night. Then we realized we had nothing to give them. Bobby popped his head over the wall again. 'Cod or skate?' he asked them.

After we'd sent out for fish and chips, Bobby disappeared into his bar and returned with a case of champagne. We washed it down with that.

On the other side lived a woman so fanatically house proud that when she held a party she would put plastic sheeting over the carpets and the food would be served in the garage. Bobby happened to be looking out of the window one day when he spotted her daily cleaner with rubber gloves and swimming costume on, scrubbing out the floor of the pool. What really caught Bobby's eye was her cellulite. Her thighs were like old bath sponges. He was transfixed, absolutely horrified. 'If you ever got like that, I'd divorce you,' he said.

I think he was half-serious. He'd been quite chubby as a child; at one stage he'd been nicknamed Tubby. He dreaded the thought of getting fat if he let himself go. He was so unbelievably disciplined about his weight and fitness that even on holiday he never let up his training routine. He hated excess weight, *hated* it – and that horror extended to me. He really did not like me to put on weight

151

and would tell me to go to the gym and work out. My getting flabby didn't tally with his ideal of everything being correct and proper.

Did that upset me? Not at all. I suppose I'm a bit that way myself. I still go to the gym, even now.

I think Bobby must have been a pioneer of the Atkins diet – except for the drink, of course, but he never worried about those calories because he could always go out and run them off. His stamina was almost superhuman. When Dean was little, Bobby would get him to accompany him on a bike when he went out running. They'd go from Chigwell to Gants Hill to Woodford and back – a round trip of some eight miles – and when Dean got tired Bobby would carry him and push the bike uphill, still running.

Dean was always proud of the way his father caused a stir wherever they went together. Sometimes he found it useful, too. At his first school he quickly showed himself to be a very good footballer and the team could often count on scoring a few extra goals because Bobby's presence on the touchline so distracted opponents.

As time went on, Stradbroke Drive developed into a real party road. Victories in a major event were celebrated at our house on a Sunday morning. Come to that, so were defeats. Further along the road lived Sue and John Braine, whose dinner party one Christmas night ended with more than a few guests deciding what a good idea it would be to drink crème de menthe out of a goldfish bowl. At the time, an ad was showing on TV depicting a labrador puppy running away with a gradually unfurling roll of Andrex, to demonstrate how long it was, so Bobby decided to test out the theory with loo paper and the Braines' dog, Fifi.

Bobby wasn't the cold, aloof figure that he's sometimes been painted. When he was with people he knew well and trusted, he was open and mischievous. The Bobby I remember is the Bobby of those years: warm, tender, teasing, with an insatiable drive to live life to the hilt and a characteristic way of laughing, almost soundlessly, with his head tipped back. When I picture him in my mind now, that's who I see.

In spite of being in the throes of moving, I made plans to watch Bobby play for England against West Germany in the quarter-final, second leg of the 1972 European Championships. Judith Hurst was going to come with me. We often travelled together to watch Geoff and Bobby. While I was away, Doss would move in to look after the children. After the rather wary relationship that we had had in the 'My Robert' days, she and I had become really close. She was very good with the children and they always liked her coming to stay.

The England match was in West Berlin and Judith and I had already booked our tickets when Alf named his squad. Bobby was in it but Geoff wasn't. We girls were loath to give up our trip, so after much persuasion a very disappointed Geoff agreed to go as a spectator. Poor man. All the big hotels in the city were full, so while Judith and I got to share a luxurious double room with a bed nearly the size of a football pitch, Geoff was relegated to a single bed in a matchbox miles away.

After watching England hold West Germany to a goalless draw, Judith, Geoff and I met up with Bobby and went out with Franz Beckenbauer and his wife. The evening finished in the small hours of the morning. Geoff set off to escort Judith back to our hotel room before going off to his lonely bachelor bed, and Bobby and I followed them on later.

Bobby by this time was in spectacularly mellow mood and it was more a question of my escorting him than the other way round. I decided he had better sober up before he presented himself at the England team hotel, so he came back with me and promptly fell onto the bed, on which Judith was already curled up fast asleep. Within seconds, so was Bobby. He was impossible to shift, so I got in between them and dozed off, too.

In the morning I was woken by the ringing of the phone. Bobby fumbled for the receiver. It was one of the FA staff. 'Is that you, Bobby? Great. We've been looking for you everywhere,' the man said. 'You'd better get a move on or you'll miss the team flight back to London.'

I sat up in the middle of the bed. Next to me, so did Judith.

'Oh, Judith!' I said. 'Good morning. Bobby, it's Judith. Say good morning to Judith.'

'Good morning, Jude,' said Bobby at his most dignified.

He went off to rejoin the squad, leaving Judith and me to pack our things before checking out. Judith was about to put some of my perfume in her case by mistake.

'Excuse *me*,' I said. 'Pinching my perfume.'

'You must be joking,' said Judith. 'I've just shared my bed with you and your husband.'

When the building of Morlands was finished and we totted up the bill, it came to roughly £80,000. In the early Seventies, that was a colossal sum and some people thought we had taken on too much. I was quite upset to see descriptions of our 'luxury' home in the papers accompanied by expressions of fear that we'd never recoup our money. Either that or we would be denounced for building it. It seemed to be standard tactics; they'd built us up and now they were going to try and knock us down.

From the point of view of Morlands itself, those who decried it couldn't have been more wrong. It was a gorgeous, glamorous house and living there was everything we dreamed it would be. But something did come along to knock us down, big time. It was another business project, the Woolston Hall Country Club.

Bobby was already gaining a reputation as someone who was unlucky in business. That wasn't completely fair. His sports goods shop opposite the West Ham ground was hugely successful. Our ventures into the property market stood us in good stead, too. In fact, we could have fared even better had we been less cautious.

In the mid-Sixties we were offered two huge houses in Kensington to buy and let, and also a row of houses across from West Ham's ground at Upton Park. We had always believed in bricks and mortar, so we wanted to go for it and have my mother manage them. Jack Turner, Bobby's agent, felt it was too expensive and far too risky. Bobby, having great faith in Jack and his business expertise, decided to err on the side of caution. I was sorry he did. But I don't want to come over as someone who with hindsight would have made a totally different decision. Most people have similar stories about The Big One That Got Away. What it shows is that Bobby didn't just throw money at things.

Saying that, in some other areas of business we weren't cautious enough. We weren't always very shrewd about what we got involved in and sometimes we were carried away by glamorous-sounding ventures.

The Woolston Hall project was a bigger risk and so potentially a bigger disaster. That didn't daunt us. Nor were we deterred by Jack Turner's misgivings. He advised Bobby and me strongly against involvement, but we were so convinced of Woolston Hall's potential that Bobby invested £5,000 and put his name to it by becoming a director.

Woolston Hall was a mansion set in twenty-six acres of

Essex countryside, close to Chigwell. It was twelve miles from the centre of London and in a catchment area which included some of the most affluent people in the south of England. The plan was to turn it into an exclusive country club. Bobby was roped in by Del Simmonds, a local businessman whose golfing partner was Sean Connery. Bobby's friend, Lou Wade, was an investor with his son, Michael, as was Kenny Bird, an East End publican. Bobby and Sean Connery were to be the front men for the operation.

The club had a restaurant, cocktail bar, lounge bar, disco, golf driving range and putting green, pool, tennis courts and hairdresser's. This was run by Sean, a former artistic director at Vidal Sassoon, and we ladies would sit under the dryers and be served drinks. No one was ever sure whether the red faces with which we emerged were because of the drinks or the hot air.

Everything at Woolston Hall had to be the best and the place was starting to look stunning when, just before the opening, Kenny Bird pulled out. A mysterious arson attempt followed that and then Del Simmonds resigned after someone fired a shotgun at his house from a passing car. The directors had already expended so much time, money and energy that the only option was to press on. The membership fee was set at £100 a year and the club opened in August 1972 with a spectacular celebrity bash in which guests were plied with caviar and champagne.

The ethos was no-expense-spared opulence and excess in

all things, from the silver teaspoons to the gold-plated taps in the cloakrooms, and each director has his own engraved solid silver goblet. The place had more kitchen staff than the Dorchester.

I was in charge of the ladies' social side and organized outings such as coach trips to Shepperton film studios, where we would capture the actors and drag them back to Woolston Hall for frivolities. Ladies' outings always finished with wonderful dinners, ordered by me at great expense and left untouched by the women because they were all on diets.

On Sunday afternoons there was a children's disco, which brought in the parents as well. That was one of the few profitable parts of the operation. It quickly came home to us that apart from the restaurant and bars, none of the other facilities brought in any revenue. At the same time, we realized some of the kitchen staff were pilfering.

Some of the mishaps had a slightly farcical quality. Lou Wade persuaded his fellow directors that they needed to make Woolston Hall more exotic, so they had a little pond put in, on which flamingos were installed. The winter of 1972 was unusually cold and the birds froze in the ice. Enormous sums of money were thus wasted and if I'd been able to see what the future held, I might have preferred our bank account to have been frozen with the flamingos.

CHAPTER TEN

A Touch of Brian

Obviously Bobby couldn't be an England player for ever. He was 33. Even so, virtually everyone in the country took it as read that England would qualify for the 1974 World Cup in West Germany. The attitude was that they were still one of the best sides in the world, with the best goalkeeper in Gordon Banks and the best captain in Bobby Moore.

Besides, if any man could put up a fight against the march of time, it was my Bobby. He had a marvellous constitution, his game had never depended on pace and he still put so much discipline and commitment into his training that he might have been an ambitious youngster trying to push his way into the first team.

He remained incredibly weight-conscious. On the occasional days when he over-indulged himself with some normally forbidden culinary delight, he would cut back totally the day after. If we were in a bar having a drink, he would count out twelve peanuts, never more, never less.

That was his ration and he was sticking to it. I, of course, finished off the rest.

As well as being so controlled and disciplined, he was also almost supernaturally strong. I think both of us believed he was invincible.

In summer 1973, England flew out behind the Iron Curtain on a tour that began with their World Cup qualifying tie against Poland. It was always going to be a huge challenge. The Polish supporters were passionate and fervent and they had jam-packed the stadium in Katowice in the hope of fireworks from Wlodi Lubanski, the quickest and deadliest striker in European football. They got what they wanted in the first few minutes of the second half.

Poland had already gone one-up with a goal that was claimed by their Number 7 although in fact the ball brushed against Bobby and spun off him into the ground before it flew up inside the near post off Peter Shilton's shoulder. No one could blame Bobby for that one. Peter was beaten and Bobby was just making the classic defender's last ditch stand. In any case, there was plenty of time left. Alf Ramsey called all the players around him at half time and said, 'Gentlemen, if we keep plugging away we'll get some sort of result. A draw at least.'

Instead, Bobby went back out and made a bad mistake straightaway. He called for the ball from Roy McFarland but Lubanski was closing on him quickly. It wasn't ever Bobby's way just to boot the ball into the stands so he glanced up to check where he wanted it to go. Lubanski pounced and took it off him to score. It put Poland two goals up and knocked the stuffing out of England. To make a bad night worse, Alan Ball was sent off.

That night in Katowice was the low point of Bobby's footballing life. Eight years before, he had been England's hero. Now, with his manager and the rest of the team, he was being pilloried in the papers. I felt so badly for him.

Normally the England team wouldn't have known about the contempt in which they were being held by the gentlemen of the press, because British newspapers never got behind the Iron Curtain and phone connections were poor. But this time the British Airways charter plane had gone back to London before the next stage of the trip. When it returned to Poland to take the team on to Moscow, the English papers were on board. The cabin crew innocently distributed them among the players, who after reading the scathing verdicts on their performance were so upset that they decided not to say any more to the press.

Somehow, Nigel Clarke had to produce Bobby's column for the *Daily Mirror*. He trudged on foot from the media hotel to England's and stood outside shouting, 'Mooro!' at the upper windows.

Eventually one of them opened, and Bobby stuck his head out.

'What am I going to put in your column?' shouted Nigel.

'Tell them I'm gutted!' shouted down the normally guarded and press-conscious Bobby, and closed the window.

Bobby's habitual insomnia kicked in during the very hot and humid nights that followed. There was no air-conditioning and after tossing and turning for a second successive night, Bobby was so fed up that he got up, tucked a newspaper under his arm and went out for a pre-dawn walk and some fresh air. After he had walked round the park for a while, he sat down on a bench and started to peer at the paper. Soon he dropped off to sleep. The next thing he knew was that the sun was shining brightly and two FA officials who had gone out for a stroll after breakfast were staring at him with outraged disbelief.

Bobby sat up, pushing aside the newspaper that had fallen across him. 'Good morning,' he said.

The officials went storming back to the hotel where one announced disgustedly, 'I've just seen our captain asleep in the park like a tramp.'

The mood in the England camp lifted a bit. The players fell about laughing when they got to hear about it. Not so the stuffy and stiff establishment characters in the FA. They didn't see the funny side at all. Neither did they know about Bobby's habit of getting up at night and wandering the streets if he couldn't sleep. They only saw the England captain asleep on a bench and were appalled. I feel sure that this was one of the reasons Bobby was excluded from the FA hierarchy after his football career was over.

After the match against the USSR, won 2–1 by England, the team went on to Turin for a friendly against Italy. It was going to be the first time Bobby had faced them and was special because it coincided with Bobby's 107th full international appearance, a record. Alf made an exception to his usual practice and announced Bobby as captain well before the team declaration. That gave Bobby the chance to receive a presentation from the press, a Capodimonte china ornament. Someone had a sense of humour – the ornament featured a tramp on a bench feeding a bird.

The match wasn't worthy of the occasion. Another mistake by Bobby led to one of Italy's goals in their defeat of England. Bobby sat up all night drinking with Alan Ball and some of the press corps. Just after six in the morning, the England amateur team came down into the foyer. They were on tour as well, and just about to set off by coach to their next fixture. Bobby sent them on their way with three bottles of champagne. No one could have known from his demeanour how much he minded the depths to which his England prospects had plunged. But behind the mask, he was distraught.

Back home in Chigwell, waiting for him to return, I wasn't completely aware at first of how badly things had gone wrong for him. In fact, I was far more preoccupied with the latest domestic crisis – Dean and Roberta had had a fight. Although Dean was younger than Roberta by three years, he was tall and strong like his daddy. Roberta, on the other hand, was small and fine-boned and she had come off the worse in their rough and tumble. Her arm was hurt and I was terrified that she had broken it. She needed to get to hospital quickly.

In the middle of this chaos, Bobby arrived. He had Alan Ball in tow. Both of them had had a few – rather more than a few, in fact.

'How could you let yourself get in such a state?' I said angrily, as he flopped into a chair in his bar. He said nothing, just leered up at me.

There wasn't time for a full scale row to develop, thank goodness – Roberta's injured arm was too important. I dashed off to casualty with her, leaving Bobby and Alan commiserating with each other.

The next day, when he'd sobered up and started talking about how badly he'd played, I wished I'd been more sympathetic. No wonder he'd got blind drunk – it was the only way he could blot out the pain.

It was rare for him to bare his soul because he was normally so good at compartmentalizing things. I realized how desperate he was feeling. He was really anxious. He was horrified by his mistake against Lubanski and kept going over it with me. He was worried that his reactions weren't so sharp and that he was slipping.

'I think I've blown my chances of ever playing for England again,' he said. 'I should have been in control of the game and I wasn't. I feel I've let everyone down – Alf, the lads, the country.'

I tried desperately to reassure him, but it was hard to reach him. Even as I reminded him of all his caps, I thought, 'What a futile exercise. He doesn't need to hear about what he's achieved in the past. He wants to know if he's still got a future.'

It was into this period of despair that Brian Clough barged.

'Is that Bobby Moore?' said the familiar nasal tones at the other end of the phone. 'Now then, young man, I hear you're interested in winning a League Championship medal.'

Brian knew exactly which buttons to push. 'Who wouldn't be?' said Bobby.

'Would you play for Derby County?'

'Yes, why not?'

'That'll do me.'

Brian and his assistant, Peter Taylor, had turned Derby County around. Although it wasn't one of the money clubs like Manchester United or Arsenal, it had won the League Championship in 1972 and Brian was still the manager of the moment. He was dashing and cavalier and he broke the rules – just the man to shake up the stuffy, creaking structure that was English football. Bobby agreed to meet Brian for lunch at the Churchill, an upmarket hotel where the Derby team stayed when they had a London game.

Bobby was there in time to witness Brian's arrival in a gold Rolls Royce. After a drink in the bar, they headed towards the dining room where the *maître d'* tried to refuse Bobby admittance because he was dressed in a casual shirt and sweater.

'My team,' said Brian to the *maître d'*, 'will never stay here again if my player can't come into this restaurant.'

'Hang on, Brian,' said Bobby. 'I'm not your player yet.'

'Shut up,' said Brian. 'You're my player. That's no trouble. I'll ring Ron Greenwood right away and sort it out.'

Bobby raised an eyebrow and followed Brian in. After they sat down to read the enormously expensive *haute cuisine* menu, Brian attracted the waiter's attention. 'Have you got any mushy peas?' he shouted.

Then he leaned across the table and fixed Bobby with a mesmerizing glare. 'I can make you play better than you've ever played,' he said.

He didn't need to say any more. Bobby was riveted.

'He must have hypnotized me,' he said when he talked it over with me later. 'All I can see is a white shirt with a ram on the chest. I love the man. I love him for wanting me.'

There would have been drawbacks to a Derby move. Either we would have to uproot the children from their schools and move as a family, or Bobby would have to

Above: Football becomes glamorous. The 'Posh 'n'
Becks' of the Sixties in Epping Forest. *Inset*: Bobby's
favourite photo of me.

Right: Our first house, Glenwood Gardens. Bobby under orders.

Below: High flyer. England training at Roehampton, July 1966.

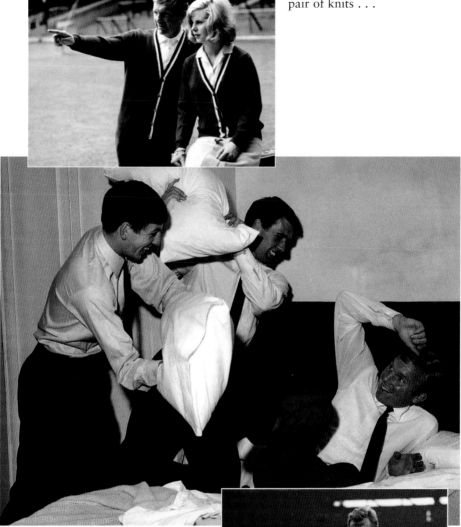

Left: Model couple. A right pair of knits . . .

Above: Hit me baby one more time? Martin Peters and Geoff Hurst indulge in some antics with Bobby ahead of an England game.

Right: Always stylish. Action from his early days as a West Ham player.

Above: What a man! I was in tears as I watched my Bobby parade the World Cup trophy at Wembley, July 1966.

Right: Forever the gent. The Queen's gloves are still spotless as Bobby receives the trophy.

Left: Banished to the Bulldog. World Cup celebrations among the wives: (from left) Mrs Moore, Peters, Hurst, Springett and Bonetti.

Above: 1965 baby boom at West Ham. From left (front): the Brabrooks, the Boyces, the Byrnes, the Hursts, the Peters, and the Sissons; (middle) the Bovingtons, the Browns and the Moores; (back) the Preslands, the Standens and the Burketts.

Above: Motorcade in Malta. Tina with the infamous red scarf.

Above: The cigar was not a patch on the joy Bobby felt at receiving the Player of the World Cup Award at a ceremonial banquet in 1966.

Left: Anyone for cricket? A change of rules for the England team.

Left: Man in Vogue. Football's first pin-up, 1962.

Right: Mixing with the stars. Bobby and Jimmy Greaves with Yul Brynner and Sean Connery during the victorious England squad's visit to Pinewood Studios in July 1966.

Below: West Ham boys letting loose: (from left) Budgie Byrne, Ron Greenwood, Peter Brabrook, Jackie Burkett, Alan 'Sammy' Sealey, Bill Jenkins, Ken Brown, and Bobby.

Left: A night on the town. With Jimmy Tarbuck and Eric Morecambe at the Anglo American Sporting Club.

Below: Bobby and his hero Frank Sinatra, in Los Angeles in the mid-Seventies.

Below: Tina, Francis Bonetti, Pepe the hotel manager, Judith Hurst and Kathy Peters in Guadalajara.

Above: Relaxing at home. Bobby the doting dad having fun with Roberta.

Right: Welcoming Dean into the world – such a joyful moment.

commute, spending part of the week in London and the rest in the Midlands.

I knew that being away from his home turf so much would be a challenge for him. He liked being in London, among his own people and close to his business interests. But all the drawbacks were outweighed by the prospect of him feeling motivated and enthusiastic again, and I was all for him accepting Brian's offer.

Ron Greenwood, unfortunately, wasn't.

Not long after the meeting at the Churchill, Brian and one of the Derby directors paid a visit to Upton Park. 'I want a chat with you,' said Brian. 'Got any whisky? I've come to take Bobby Moore off your hands.'

'No chance whatsoever,' said Ron.

'I'll give you £400,000 if you throw Trevor Brooking in as well.'

'You can't be serious,' said Ron.

'Every man's got his price,' said Brian.

'There's no point going on,' said Ron. 'They're not available, Brian. But I'll pass your offer on to the board.'

Needless to say, both Bobby and Trevor Brooking stayed at West Ham.

Would going to Derby have brought Bobby that Championship medal? Brian was a specialist at bringing the best out of players who were past their first youth and if he had stayed at Derby instead of resigning after a fall-out with the board in October, it might well have done. Instead, Brian went on, via Brighton and Leeds, to achieve great things with Nottingham Forest.

Brian's own football career had been cut short at 29 and I think that fed his ability to resurrect careers that seemed to be over. In spite of his brash, abrasive reputation, he had a huge streak of compassion. He knew what it was like to feel written off and how unfair it was when you had so much left to give. He really understood how crestfallen Bobby was about his declining career. Even though the move never happened, just knowing that Brian admired him and wanted him gave Bobby a huge boost of confidence.

When Brian died after a long period of illness in October 2004, the game lost one of its most original, dynamic figures. As a motivator of players he was exceptional, winning the European Cup, forerunner of the Champions League, twice with Forest.

Brian had his demons and in later years a drink problem forced his premature retirement, but he was a good man and he touched Bobby's life in a very positive way.

CHAPTER ELEVEN

Calling Time

Bobby spent the rest of summer 1973 sweating on his England future. The next international wasn't until September. That was a friendly against Austria at Wembley. The month after that, Poland were coming over for their return World Cup qualifying tie on 16 October.

Alf named Bobby in his squad for the Austria and Poland games. One factor which gave Bobby heart was that the squad also included Alan Ball, even though his sending off in Katowice meant he wouldn't be eligible to play in the Poland match. 'Maybe that means Alf's still including all the players he expects to field in the Finals,' said Bobby to me. He was looking for every sign of hope, however miniscule.

Determined to re-establish himself by having a good game against Austria, he went off to the England get-together. The squad based themselves in a Hertfordshire hotel and trained at the nearby sports ground in Stevenage.

One morning, when the squad were getting back into the team coach after training, Alf found his way to Bobby and sat down next to him. 'It was like when he sat down next to me after his first ever match in charge,' Bobby told me afterwards. 'But this time I knew I wasn't going to like what I was hearing.'

'I'm sorry, Bobby,' Alf said to him awkwardly. 'This is going to be disappointing for you, but you won't be playing against Austria. I'm giving Norman Hunter a game. This is the only chance to try things out and get a settled team before Poland.'

'Are you saying you don't need me any more?' said Bobby. 'If so, tell me. I don't want to hang around on the fringes embarrassing everybody. I'd rather we called it quits right now.'

'That isn't what I'm saying,' said Alf quietly. 'If we qualify for West Germany, I'll want you to captain the squad.'

'OK,' said Bobby. 'I'd better start battling to get back in the side, then.'

Martin Peters captained England against Austria. They won 7–0, England's biggest margin of victory for many years, so it wasn't a surprise when Alf kept the same side against Poland. Norman Hunter took Bobby's place at Wembley and Bobby was named as substitute. It was a crucial night for England's World Cup hopes. They had to win to qualify for the 1974 Finals. Poland only needed not to lose.

I felt so torn that I couldn't bear to watch the game on television but after a while found myself fiddling with the dial on the radio, trying to tune in to the BBC commentary. 'The most important thing is that England win. It doesn't matter who's in the side,' I lied to myself. Even so, when I found out that the score was one goal each with a few minutes to go, I started dreaming of a Roy of the Rovers scenario. A huge roar would come from the crowd as Bobby leapt off the bench and with one inch-perfect pass sent Martin Peters off on a run down the wing. Somehow, in the space of a few seconds, a familiar blond head would then pop up to beat Tomaszewski with that rarest of events, a Bobby Moore goal. The tide would have turned for England. Bobby's performance of a lifetime.

That never happened. The score stayed 1–1 to the end. For the first time, England had failed to qualify for the World Cup.

To be honest, that wasn't my primary concern. My feelings and loyalties were all for Bobby and I just hoped and prayed he would get his place back in the team.

The wish was fulfilled, if only for one game. A month after the Poland match, Italy came to England for a friendly. Alf brought Bobby back into the side so he could earn his 108th cap and finish his England career at Wembley. He never played for his country again and six months later, in May 1974, Alf was sacked by the FA. He and Bobby had been at the forefront of England's greatest football era. That was over now.

With the worst possible timing, the end of Bobby's England career coincided with the end of Woolston Hall. It had run rapidly into debt and with hindsight, I can't believe how naïve we were. Woolston Hall was a fabulous place, but probably a bit ahead of its time. Even so, if we had been a little more sensible and a lot wiser, it could have done brilliantly well. The problem was that no one on the board of directors really knew what they were doing. There was no one with any experience of the catering industry or expertise in running that kind of venture.

The directors issued more shares without success and as the club got more and more into debt, Bobby's agents took on increased guarantees at the bank. Last-ditch attempts were made to turn the place around by cutting prices at the expense of exclusivity but by early 1974, the directors realized that the best solution was to cut their losses and close.

Woolston Hall taught Bobby a very hard lesson – just how hard we didn't find out until a little later, when he discovered that as alleged guarantor he was going to be sued for the six-figure sum still owing. He went up to London to discuss things with the bank, and when he came back his face was grey. I grabbed his hand. 'We'll get through this,' I said. 'We can trade down. I'll go out to work.'

'I don't want you to work,' said Bobby brusquely. 'It's my job to keep you. Anyway, what would you do? I'll have to find something, somehow.'

Bobby wasn't really thinking straight around that time. He suddenly decided that instead of selling Morlands and trading down, we ought to move to an even bigger house, way out in the country. I played along with his idea for a while because it seemed important to give him something else to focus on, and we came very close to buying a country mansion. But I didn't want to move there and in the end fate helped me out.

We were on a promotional trip to Saint Lucia when we woke up one night to see three men in the process of ransacking our room of all our money and jewellery. Bobby chased after them, but thank God he didn't catch them up; one had a machete. The experience was terrifying. Even if I'd been keen on moving to that remote place in the country, the robbery in Saint Lucia would have put me off, and Bobby felt the same.

Woolston Hall didn't put Bobby off the idea of being a man of business. His next venture was to become co-owner of five pubs with our friend and neighbour, Jimmy Quill. Jimmy already owned the Blind Beggar, the East End pub once notorious for being where Ronnie Kray shot George Cornell. Mooro's was in Stratford; Georgie Best came to the opening with the stunning Angie, and the place flourished.

The other pubs weren't so successful. They didn't lose money, but neither did they make as much as Bobby had hoped, at a time when he was already feeling dogged by misfortune. The situation was awkward, too. Jimmy was disappointed by Bobby's input – he wanted more from him than celebrity appearances. Bobby, for his part, was upset about money. 'Can you sort it out with Jimmy?' he said to me. 'You get on better with people.'

I tried to help because I understood how Bobby worried about offending people and letting them down; that was why he sometimes pushed me to the forefront. He was an interesting mixture of contrasts, really. In his own milieu, negotiating about money with Ron Greenwood, for instance, he was steely and calculating. But Bobby was a different character when he strayed outside football. He lost all his confidence. He was good at making money, but he wasn't good *with* it. He was only in his early thirties and he didn't come from a world where people were used to money. His father was a gas-fitter. He would look at someone who appeared to be plausible and believe what he was hearing. But I admired the way he kept on trying.

I don't know if any of the other directors or people involved with Woolston Hall had to repay any of the six-figure debt, or if, in fact, Bobby was the sole guarantor for the sum involved. I only know that being the honourable man he was, he had to honour his commitment, and it was a colossal burden.

'Will we have to declare ourselves bankrupt?' I asked.

'No, but it's going to cost us all our savings and I'm going to have to work for God knows how long to pay it back,' he said.

But at least another club was ready to give him a job.

CHAPTER TWELVE

Extra Time

Bobby's last senior game for West Ham was in January 1974, when he twisted his knee ligaments during an FA Cup game against Hereford United. He was carried off and out for eight weeks and his replacement, Mick McGiven, did well enough in the celebrated Number 6 shirt to help lift West Ham away from relegation trouble. Bobby had his ticket out.

Ron Greenwood called him into his office. 'All right,' he said. 'You can go. But we want £25,000 for you.'

'Wait a minute,' said Bobby. 'You agreed at the start of the season that I could leave on a free at the end.'

'The board are insisting on a fee,' said Ron.

Bobby couldn't believe it. 'West Ham signed me for nothing as an apprentice,' he said to me. 'They've had sixteen years of service out of me. I should be being let go for nothing so I can get the best possible contract for myself at a new club. Instead of that, I'm being used to balance the club books.'

Even so, £25,000 was a bargain price for an England captain. Bobby also knew he only had one or two seasons of high earning left in league football, so he played hard to get. Two First Division clubs, Stoke and Leicester, were interested. So were Norwich, at the time still in the First Division but doomed to relegation at the end of the 1973–74 season.

Going to Norwich would have reunited Bobby with John Bond, now the manager of the East Anglian club. Muffin was so keen to have him that he said Bobby could stay in London, train with West Ham and commute on match days. But Bobby didn't think retaining the link with West Ham was a good idea. 'I want to go somewhere new,' he said. 'I want a change of atmosphere, so I can make a complete break with the past.'

That didn't extend to rubbing West Ham out of his life altogether. Malcolm Allison, his first mentor at West Ham, was now managing Crystal Palace and Bobby hoped an offer would come in from Selhurst Park. But with 14 March, the deadline day for Football League transfers, looming, Big Mal was uncharacteristically silent. Instead, on 13 March, Bobby received an approach from Alec Stock at Fulham.

Alec was a soft-spoken West Countryman with the knack of getting the best out of smaller clubs. Bobby had always liked him. Ron Greenwood was a football perfectionist but you couldn't touch the soul of the man, whereas

Alec was a kindly man, easy-going and approachable. That was the difference. Although he wasn't a bit like Malcolm Allison in other ways, he had the gregariousness that Bobby was drawn to. That was why he admired and respected Brian Clough – the man had such enthusiasm. It was a dimension that Ron lacked.

Even so, Bobby was still determined to take it to the wire. 'I'll sleep on it,' he told Alec.

For Alec it was time to put Plan B into action. One of Fulham's players was Bobby's former England team-mate, Alan Mullery. Bobby had a great liking for Alan, who after a successful spell at Spurs had come back to Fulham, the club of his early years, to see out his playing days.

The next day, Bobby emerged from an early morning training session at Upton Park to find Alan waiting with a handful of paperwork. 'Morning, Bob,' said Alan. 'Glad you're coming to Fulham. You'll love it, it's different class. Just sign here.'

Alec had despatched him and Graham Hortop, the Fulham secretary, to West Ham with the instructions not to leave until Bobby's signature was on the transfer documents.

Bobby's final game for West Ham was in the reserves, but hundreds of supporters gathered to say goodbye to the man whose career at Upton Park had started with the West Ham Colts on 6 October 1956. His first team debut was on 8 September 1958, against Manchester United, and he captained West Ham in their FA Cup victory over Preston in 1964 and in their European Cup winners Cup win against TSV Munich 1860 in 1965. On 17 February 1973 he exceeded the record 509 appearances made for West Ham by Jimmy Ruffell. As England captain he had brought lustre to the club.

Sadly, Ron Greenwood's farewell was grudging.

'Are you sorry Bobby's leaving?' a TV reporter asked him.

Ron stuck out his chin. 'I'm sorry when any player leaves,' he said.

In 1974, long before the era of Mohammed al Fayed, Craven Cottage was a cosy place. One of its distinguishing features was a balcony complete with wrought iron balustrade where you could take tea like Edwardian ladies and gentlemen. The club had known better times but it boasted some famous Old Boys. Bobby's boyhood hero, Johnny Haynes – the Maestro – spent his entire first class career there between 1952 and 1970. George Cohen, Bobby's World Cup-winning team-mate, played alongside Johnny in the Sixties and, like Alan Mullery, Rodney Marsh had started his playing career there. For a long time its chairman had been Tommy Trinder, an amiable stand-up comedian of his day. His act featured a lot of self-deprecating Fulham jokes.

Bobby signed for Fulham on a Friday and played his

first game for them on the following Tuesday, 19 March 1974. His debut attracted three times the normal crowd. Unfortunately, Fulham's opponents that night were Middlesbrough, Second Division leaders by a gulf as wide as Mexico's. By the time they won the Second Division title two months later, they were 15 points ahead of the rest – at a time when two points, not three were awarded for a victory. Bobby's new club helped them generously on their way. Fulham were 4–0 down after twenty minutes.

'I think I might have made a mistake coming here,' murmured Bobby to Alan Mullery as they trudged away from the goalmouth for the fourth time.

But Bobby's first full season there, the 1974–75 one, was magical. His presence seemed to inspire the other players and the side lifted their game. In May they found them-selves travelling to Wembley for the FA Cup Final. Almost predictably, a twist of fate made sure their opponents were West Ham. Roberta, Dean and I dressed up in Fulham colours for the day and if Fulham's Cup run had been a movie, it would have ended with Bobby lifting the trophy. Real life never was like that, and West Ham won 2–0.

But Fulham had booked the Dorchester, win or lose, for a party that night. It was so good that even some of the West Ham players, who had been celebrating nearby at the Grosvenor in Park Lane, turned up. James Mason, who was staying at the Dorchester, talked his way into the banquet and asked if he could join us. I thought that was incredible. A film star had asked if he could join Bobby, not the other way round.

One of the great things about football in the mid-Seventies was the way the game was developing in the US. For players like Bobby, that meant a hugely enjoyable way to extend their playing days because the North American Soccer League relied heavily on big name talent from all over the world to draw in the crowds.

Bobby had just finished his second season with Fulham when we went out to spend the summer of 1976 with San Antonio Thunder in Texas. Bobby had been asked to guest there as player and coach and didn't need any prompting to say yes. He and I both loved the States. We thought New York was the best place we'd ever been.

The first time we went there was with West Ham, who were playing in a cup competition and had given the players the choice of extra pay or taking their wives on the trip. I was about to turn 21 when that happened. Visiting New York was my biggest ambition. We flew BOAC from London via Prestwick and Bangor, Maine – it took twelve hours. In those days you got dressed up to fly and I had my photo taken at Heathrow, wearing dark glasses and a white suit. When I saw it later in the paper I thought how starry and mysterious I looked.

That first trip had its awkward moments. The girls were very young and many of them had no experience of long distance travel. Some of them fell out with each other or went around in floods of tears because they were homesick. Others managed to get as far as visiting the Empire State Building but they didn't go up – they just stood outside and looked! For Bobby and me, though, it was love at first sight. We were knocked out by everything, from the enormous portions of strawberry shortcake to swimming at Coney Island to the musical toilet seat covers. We travelled on the subway, where I was mesmerized by a giant nun who suddenly started spitting. I looked more closely and noticed that the 'nun' was wearing great big men's boots. That was definitely an encounter I would never have had in Ilford.

My mother had given Bobby enough money to organize a 21st birthday treat for me. It took place at the Latin Quarter, where Al Martino was in cabaret. He was a huge star in the early Sixties and all of us girls were big fans. It was the highlight of the evening when Al strolled around the tables, singing.

He seemed to stop an unusually long time at our table and a little while after that, a waiter approached me with a message. 'Mr Martino would like to take you out to dinner,' he said.

I was unbelievably flattered and it was with the greatest regret that I told him, 'Sorry, but I'm with my husband.'

But the next night, there came a knock on my bedroom door. I opened it to see a waiter carrying a tray on which there was a bottle of champagne and a note. It read:

'Mr Martino will be pleased to drink this with you after tonight's show.'

I gasped. I was absolutely flummoxed. 'But – but – ,' I stammered.

It was only when I peered more closely at the waiter that I recognized Alan Sealey. It was a tease.

That was a fantastic introduction to the States, and Bobby and I dreamed we'd go back for longer some day. Bobby's spell with San Antonio gave us the chance. That summer of 1976 was one of the happiest times we'd ever had. Far away from England and the financial problems left by Woolston Hall, he was a different person, carefree and full of fun.

I had to wait for the start of the school holidays before I joined him there with Roberta and Dean and the moment he saw me, he said, 'My Princess has arrived.' It was wonderful to meet up with him there. Our living accommodation was a cathedral-style house with high, lofted ceilings. I was surprised by how homely and welcoming Bobby had made it look. He had filled it with flowers. They weren't just thrown into vases, either. I had recently done a flower arranging course and multi-talented Bobby had clearly picked up some hints.

My first sight of him on Texan soil was with a voluptuous strawberry blonde clinging to his arm. She had the face of a naughty angel and the body of Dolly Parton. Bobby introduced her as Annie Semple, wife of the Rangers

183

goalie, Billy. Like Bobby, Billy was a big name veteran spending the summer with San Antonio Thunder. The evening had just started and Annie, who spoke in a broad Scots accent, was on her best behaviour. She ordered 'a wee sherry', which she drank with her little finger crooked. Inevitably, one wee sherry was followed by another, until by the end of the evening she was on her hands and knees by the coffee table, checking that the sambuccas were level. Then she chased a woman out of the room who had come up to ask Bobby for his autograph. She was madly in love with Bobby and still is to this day. We had such fun hanging out with her and Billy.

That San Antonio trip was idyllic. They were lovely, chilled out times. No one knew us so we could go out as a normal family. We could spend hours on the beach at Corpus Christi with no one to pester Bobby by asking where he'd hidden the bracelet.

There was one very tiny fly in the ointment. The club owner was the boss of Braniff Airlines and when the players ran out onto the pitch to the tune of 'The Yellow Rose Of Texas', they had to wear stetsons and carry yellow roses. You can imagine how much the stylish, immaculate Bobby enjoyed that. On the credit side, we were deluged with free tickets and passes for places like Taco Bell. Dean picked up fifty-four. Off he went to the restaurant to claim his free tacos, all fifty-four of them. That must have been some sort of record.

While Bobby was out training, I'd go to the gym with the Southern belles. Our babysitter was a long-haired, guitar-playing hippie called Zak and the summer days just slid dreamily into each other ... trying to catch fireflies, Bobby and Dean playing golf, Roberta going to school wearing a long dress. Annie Semple gave Roberta her first babysitting job, looking after little Scott and Lee. Roberta was terribly excited – twelve years old and convinced she was babysitter *extraordinaire*. We made lifelong friends and it was bliss. There was even a possibility of Bobby going on to join a club in Hawaii as head coach.

Bliss was short-lived. We had to cut the trip short because Bobby's father, Big Bob, had been rushed into hospital with a stroke. It was difficult getting flights out with the children at short notice. We'd had such a marvellous time and it was such a sad reason to be leaving. Once again we left the US, telling ourselves we'd go back.

Back in England, the 1976–77 season was just starting and there was a new face at Fulham. With that dark, curly hair and those sparkling blue, almond-shaped eyes, Georgie Best really was Gorgeous George. He was quiet and skinny but cheeky and flirty with it. He had charisma and a fabulous dress sense, and you could tell he loved the women. It dripped from every pore. All the girls who met him fell a little bit in love with him. He was a delight, but what really gave him his appeal was his air of vulnerability. He was a little boy lost.

Bobby and I used to bump into him at Tramp, where he'd have the Miss World *du saison* in tow. The first time I met him, I said, 'Oh, Georgie, I hear you go after all the girls.'

'If you were on your own, I'd be after you,' he said.

'Watch it, Georgie,' said Bobby, but he was laughing.

Bobby really liked Georgie. They were a little bit alike in that they both had that mysterious X-factor. You can't define it except to say that it bestows star quality and Bobby and Georgie identified it in each other. Whenever they were together, it was like a meeting of the Mutual Admiration Society.

One of the funniest encounters with George was when Bobby and I went to dinner at Ned Sherrin's. Ned was the producer of *Till Death Us Do Part*, and among the guests was Johnny Speight, creator, as the show's scriptwriter, of the legendary Alf Garnett. We got to know him when Bobby appeared as himself in one of the episodes.

Georgie was also expected at Ned's, but most of the dinner had been eaten when he arrived – in the state of wear for which he was celebrated. We were drinking sambuccas, complete with floating coffee beans and flaming glasses, by that time and I think that for Georgie they were the straw that broke the camel's back because he only had one before he fell into a deep sleep.

'Look at George,' said Johnny. 'All the world's greatest players failed to stop him, but sambucca left him for dead.'

'That's a marvellous story for my column,' said Bobby.

Shortly afterwards, Bobby wrote in the *Daily Mirror*, 'The only time I've ever seen George Best completely beaten was by Sam Booka.' It created a huge stir among the press, who were all asking who this Sam Booka was and what club he played for.

Another great friend of Bobby's to join him at Craven Cottage at the start of the 1976–77 season was Rodney Marsh. Rodney was like George Best in some ways. He was lovable while having a bit of devilment about him. He could best be summed up by saying he was naughty in the nicest possible way. He had flair and style and was a bit off the wall, but at the same time he was thoughtful and really kind. Roberta and Dean adored him. They loved it when he came to our house because of those treasure hunts he organized for them. Jean, his wife, was lovely, too.

The presence of Georgie and Bobby at Fulham meant a champagne-fuelled season. But sadly, midway through it, Alec Stock left. There had been changes at boardroom level when the club got into financial difficulties over the building of a new riverside stand. Tommy Trinder lost his fight to keep control of the club and it was taken over by Ernie Clay, a pugnacious Yorkshireman. His arrival was followed soon after by Alec's departure.

Ernie Clay had been brought to Fulham by another

director, Sir Eric Miller, whose purportedly dubious business dealings were later the subject of an investigation by the Fraud Squad. He had always idolized Bobby and when the investigation became public knowledge, he called round to see us at Morlands. It was nine o'clock in the morning. 'I want you to know that all my dealings with you have been completely honest and above board,' he said.

He was in such a shaky and agitated state that Bobby really felt for him. 'Come on in and have a drink,' he said.

'No, thank you,' said Sir Eric. 'I never touch the stuff until after dark.'

Bobby said to me, 'Close the curtains, Teen, and pour the man a drink.'

It was two days afterwards that Sir Eric committed suicide. I think he had come round to say goodbye to Bobby.

The 1976–77 season was Bobby's last in English football and on 4 May he played his final home game for Fulham, against Leyton Orient. It was also his 999th League match. Billy and Annie Semple came to stay for the occasion, with Annie proudly presenting us with a black pudding which had travelled all the way from Scotland with her and which she insisted was a noted Scottish delicacy.

Fulham won 6–1 and after Bobby had done his lap of honour round Craven Cottage, everyone piled into the players' lounge to make a fuss of him. That felt really good after the low-key way in which he'd left West Ham. The celebrations carried on throughout the weekend. That evening fourteen of us, players and wives, went to Trattoria Terrazza. Bobby decided we had to have a whistling competition (won by Annie Semple) and the next day we held a retirement party at Morlands. Jimmy and Pauline Tarbuck and Kenny Lynch were among the lucky guests who got to sample Annie's black pudding.

The following week, Bobby couldn't resist turning out for Fulham's final game of the season, at Blackburn on 14 May 1977, to make it his 1,000th first class appearance. We took Doss with us and there were tears. It was nostalgic, and Doss's life wasn't easy by then. She was nursing Big Bob at home after his stroke.

Big Bob was ill for a long time and the stroke left him with impaired eyesight and very limited speech. In fact, one of the few words he could say was 'Balls', which shocked Doss terribly because Big Bob had never sworn before. Doss was so worried about Big Bob letting rip in company that she had started doing all the talking for both of them. Not long before the Blackburn game, I went to visit them with a Dutch friend, Fanny, who was determined to practise her conversational English on my in-laws. Every time Fanny spoke to Big Bob, Doss, on tenterhooks in case the B-word was uttered, answered for him.

189

Finally we got up to leave. That was when a voice said, 'Goodbye, Fanny.'

'My goodness,' said Fanny. 'He can speak.'

I looked at Big Bob and saw the old twinkle in his eye.

CHAPTER THIRTEEN

The Job That Never Was

Bobby and I were sad that his football career was to all intents and purposes over, but we felt excited, too. Between that home game against Leyton Orient and the match at Blackburn, something had happened to make us believe that he was on the brink of a marvellous new challenge. I had no idea that it would shift our lives in another direction entirely.

The first time I met Elton John was after one of his stage shows at the Roundhouse. Annie Semple and I sat next to his mum during the performance and afterwards we went backstage and then on to his birthday party. I was thrilled when Elton came over and asked Bobby and me to join him at the top table. Soon after, I found myself in animated conversation with him – about contact lenses.

I am very myopic. That's why I always remember how people walk. When I was in my teens I was never able to make out faces until their owners were practically standing on my toes. I couldn't even be certain of identifying Bobby if he was standing across the street from me. People used to mutter 'Here comes the Queen' when I approached, because I didn't acknowledge them and they thought I was sailing past with my nose in the air. They couldn't know that, far too vain to wear my glasses, I didn't recognize them because I only saw a blurred outline.

To overcome the problem, I learnt to work out who people were by the way they moved. Bobby, naturally, was easy to spot because he walked so distinctively, with short, quick steps. But it wasn't the ideal solution, and it was only when my vision was transformed with contact lenses that I could gaily trip about the place without worrying about snubbing my friends.

Most people who have contacts will have had at least one bad experience, ranging from grovelling around the carpet for a dropped lens to an emergency dash to the optician to remove a broken one from the eye. My nightmare started when I woke up with my own personal light show in one eye, accompanied by excruciating pain. Bobby rushed me to Moorfields Eye Hospital, where I discovered I had scratched the cornea. As the solution in which I'd kept the lenses had been contaminated, my eye had become infected and set up a violent reaction.

In fact, the consultant told Bobby that if he hadn't been so prompt in getting me treated, the eye might have had to be removed. As I staggered home, wearing a very fetching eye-patch under dark glasses and reflecting on how I could have been Lord Nelson on a permanent basis, I was in fairly deep shock. Barely able to see, I couldn't do anything around the house so Bobby offered to cook supper. 'What would you like?' he asked.

Bobby's culinary repertoire was limited, but he had one or two *specialités du chef*. Often when we returned home from an evening out he would head for the kitchen to make fluffy scrambled eggs. These would be served with a glass of crème de menthe, poured, whatever state he was in, with accuracy and perfection.

This was not the occasion for crème de menthe. 'Oxtail stew,' I said tremulously, 'with pearl barley in it.'

It took Bobby a while to track down the pearl barley. It had been stuck in the back of the kitchen cupboard for years. When he opened the container, its contents seemed to be moving as it was obviously providing a home for every mite in Essex. That was the end of that particular Gary Rhodes turn.

It was soon after the episode of the contact lenses that we went to the Elton John concert. Little did I know the role that he was unwittingly to play in what was probably the biggest disappointment in Bobby's life.

It was a foregone conclusion that Bobby would go into management. He'd been captain of England. He had knowledge and experience and wanted to give back to the game. His relationship with Ron Greenwood might have

ended in mutual alienation, but Bobby readily acknowledged all he had learnt from him about the game and how
it should be played.

The situation was given added urgency because of our
involvement with Woolston Hall. He was still struggling
to pay off the debt. He was no longer a League footballer.
He had to get a job. Fast.

The timing of Elton John's approach was perfect. He
had gained control of Watford, which had been bump-
ing around in the lower divisions for years. Now he was
looking for a new manager to take the club out of Division
Four.

Just after Bobby's last home game with Fulham, he
and Elton met for lunch in London. The two of them got
on well and Bobby was excited by Watford's potential. It
wasn't a big club, but Bobby was intrigued by the challenge and enthused by Elton John's ambition to turn
it into one of the big names of football. The marketing
possibilities of Elton and Bobby working together were
immense as well. Bobby and Elton discussed terms, shook
hands and arranged to meet again the following week with
their financial advisors to finalize and sign a contract.

On the day they were due to meet, Elton asked if the
lunch could be postponed for a day or two while he put
his board of directors in the picture. After that, everything
went quiet. We were due to go to Majorca on holiday and
by the time we set off, Bobby still hadn't heard anything.

Even so, he was buoyant and had a real sense that his career was moving into a fulfilling new phase. One night, soon after we arrived, he said, 'Shall we have another baby?'

The question startled me a bit. We were a close knit, loving family and I was surprised but happy that he should want a third child, but on the other hand I wasn't sure it was a good idea. 'I don't know,' I said honestly. 'I need to think about it.'

My misgivings were down to the fact that Roberta was nearly in her teens and soon Dean would be, too. I'd loved all the stages of development they'd gone through and adored being a mother, but Bobby and I had been very much hands-on parents with all the demands that entailed. Now they were less dependent on our full-time presence and I was looking forward to Bobby and me having more time together as a couple. I'd also been a full-time wife and mother since my early twenties. It had been great but I felt I had reached the stage when I needed to get out into the world and find out what I was capable of.

Another baby. Why now? I wondered. With hindsight, I think he found the future suddenly seemed very promising after three years of coping with money troubles and the decline of his playing career. He was making a fresh start and the idea of another baby tied in with this sense of a new life for us all.

What happened next put all thoughts of shall-we, shan't-we out of our minds.

Bobby always stuck to the same fitness routine, even on holiday. He would go out running and on the way back he would collect the English newspapers from the general store to read over breakfast. One morning, he came back in and silently handed me a paper. I could tell from his face that something horrible must have happened. He was absolutely white. I looked down at the paper, which was folded over to display the back page headline. Watford had announced their new manager – Graham Taylor.

I gasped and flung down the paper, but when I looked around Bobby had disappeared. He had obviously gone to lick his wounds. I ran to find him. 'Bobby, what are we going to do?' I said. 'It must be a mistake.'

Bobby was lost for words. All the breath seemed to have been knocked out of him and his hands were shaking. At last he said, 'We shook hands. I thought it was a done deal.'

I just couldn't believe it. Bobby hadn't had an inkling that this was going to happen. I felt so upset for him, and so angry that he had to find out in that dreadful way. That night I tried to lift him, telling him that everything happened for the best, but I knew that nothing I could say would ease the disappointment and hurt he was feeling.

He wanted to go home immediately. 'If I'm not going to Watford, I've got to get something else as soon as possible,' he said.

'Look, Bobby, you need breathing space,' I said. 'I think you should stay here and give yourself a few days to get over the shock. Then you can get moving on another job.'

We saw the holiday through to the end but it was desperately hard for him. He withdrew into himself and I had to hold him together. He had been looking forward to the job so much. He and Elton John were two giants of their respective professions and they had really clicked.

What went wrong? Perhaps they both got a bit carried away at that meeting and later Elton realized that he didn't want to be rushed into so big a decision. Perhaps his board persuaded him to go for a more experienced manager. Obviously he could have had no idea how much it meant to Bobby. Possibly Bobby should have been forewarned when that second meeting was postponed and he heard nothing else. But it was another cruel lesson for him.

He never found out why he didn't get that job. On the face of it he just accepted what had happened, but he was terribly hurt.

Some time later, when we were driving through the West End, a big black car slowed down beside us. There was Elton John. He wound down the window and called, 'Hi, Bobby.'

Bobby acknowledged him politely, even warmly. He couldn't show anger; he was too proud. But I knew how he felt.

The job that never happened was a pivotal event in his life.

We had to put it behind us and move on. The big question was, Where to? At first Bobby made clear to everyone that he was looking for work and applied to fill several managerial vacancies. When he received knockback after knockback, he became more and more anxious and subdued.

Once, towards the end of his playing days, Bobby and I had travelled to Brazil. I remember nothing about the trip itself or why we had been invited out there, but one thing I will never forget. On the return flight to London, with the lights dimmed and most of the passengers dozing, Bobby suddenly let out a blood-curdling scream that woke everyone around him. He didn't know he'd done it – he was having a nightmare. At the time he wouldn't say what it was about, but later he told me that the nightmare was a recurring one. 'I'm running in sand,' he said. 'I can't get anywhere.'

Now the nightmare was happening for real. There was a general assumption that Bobby was holding out for a top club, although he had already shown that he was willing to start at the bottom. I couldn't understand why he wasn't being given a chance. He was getting by with making personal appearances, but it was a proper role he wanted. As the months rolled past and still nothing came in, the newspapers took up the theme. Everyone was asking the same question: What's wrong with Bobby Moore? I, like the rest of England, had no idea. Nor did he.

In the autumn, Pele sent us two first class tickets to New York with an invitation to be guests of honour at his farewell game for New York Cosmos. We stayed at the Plaza and the whole trip really lifted our spirits. At the retirement banquet the company was stellar, with Henry Kissinger, Andy Warhol and Robert Redford among the guests, but the best thing was the way Pele spoke so warmly and respectfully about Bobby in his farewell speech. He called him 'the English gentleman who is my friend.'

Back home, we tried to make Christmas as much fun as possible for the children's sake, even though Bobby was getting increasingly despondent. It wasn't until the following spring that a job offer came his way. Unbelievably, that didn't even come from an English club.

Herning was a club in the Danish Third Division and they wanted Bobby to be their player-coach. The contract was fairly open-ended and the facilities very basic, but Bobby was just pleased to be starting his managerial career at last. He was paid on a match-to-match basis and started flying out to Denmark at weekends. The fact that England's World Cup winning captain had taken charge was huge news. A big crowd turned up for his first game, although Bobby was slightly aghast that they were separated from the pitch by nothing more permanent than ropes.

Typically, he arrived home after that first weekend laden with presents. For me there were two scarves plaited together to make a rather glamorous bandana. As soon as my friend Anita saw how it looked, she asked Bobby to bring a dozen more back for her to sell.

At first Bobby was keen for me to go out with him so that I could explore the Tivoli Gardens and some of Denmark's other famous sights. Then, as the weeks wore on and the crowds dwindled to almost nothing, he began to feel embarrassed. Clearly he no longer had novelty value, and he didn't want me to see what a hopeless cause he had taken on. He also realized that his weekly pay cheque was crippling the club's finances and that there was nothing left over to improve the team or the ground. When Harry Redknapp invited him to spend the summer working with him at Seattle Sounders in the North American Soccer League, he very quickly said yes.

I flew out with the children to join Bobby in Seattle once the school holidays started. It was a wonderful family trip, with boat rides on lakes surrounded by inspiring scenery, and walking and hiking along the tracks to Mount Rainier, snow-capped and breathtaking. We camped out at a hippy commune and chilled out over barbecues with a few beers, aspiring to be hippies ourselves, at one with nature. To this end Bobby wore the cap that I had bought him, red and white with a white pom-pom. He loved that cap, teaming it with a blue and white singlet, cut-off jeans and sandals and really fancying himself as laid back. I entered into the *zeitgeist* with flared jeans and flowing crêpe tops and one of the players' wives, a former hairdresser, plaited Roberta's hair and entwined it with ribbons and flowers. The only member of the Moore family who declined to join in the fun was Dean, who was mortified by our attempts to be flower children and looked on with utter disdain.

I loved being out there. We had no major triumphs or disasters, just a fantastic time with great friends. The only problem was that it was all too short. From the time we returned from Seattle to the very end of the following year, Bobby existed in a kind of limbo. Those two years, 1978 and 1979, were terrible for Bobby. They were such a painful contrast to the golden days of success, of being lauded and feted everywhere and of being the most famous, glamorous England player of them all.

Enough promotional work and personal appearances came his way to tide us over, but it was a struggle. We stopped being able to have spontaneous fun as a couple and as a family, and it was difficult to make arrangements too far into the future in case we couldn't afford to fulfil them when the time came.

Many couples know how money problems can temporarily erode all the joy and excitement from a marriage and sometimes even destroy it. Bobby and I weren't special in our plight and as far as I was concerned, I was with him

201

and for him whether he had money or not. To me the important thing was our love for each other and the children. But what made it really awful for him was the feeling that the world of football had cast him into darkness. His mood became increasingly morose and remote. One night he took me out to dinner and the first thing he did was order champagne. As soon as the bottle arrived, he poured two glasses. 'Tina, I love you,' he said. 'You're my Princess and you deserve the finest things in life but I can't do that any more. I can't afford it.'

I hadn't expected him to say anything like that and I felt absolutely heartbroken. His spirit seemed to have been crushed. 'Bobby, what on earth are you talking about?' I said. 'I love *you*. I don't care about champagne. I don't need expensive things. Let's sell Morlands, if that's what it takes. I don't mind where we live, I just want to be with you and the children.'

Of course it would have been a wrench to sell Morlands, but I meant what I said. That would have been better than taking Roberta and Dean out of their public schools, where they were both settled and happy with plenty of friends. Bobby and I were united in not wanting that. The two of us were grammar school educated, but the system had changed enormously since our teens and we had a lot of misgivings about the relatively new comprehensive system. Besides, Bobby was an East London boy who had done well for himself and he was proud of his children. He wanted them to have the best chance in life and in those days that meant a public school education. He was determined that they wouldn't have to suffer because of his money troubles.

I kept wishing I was able to contribute more financially. I hated the idea of his taking another lowly job and feeling miserable. By then, I could see what a very big part of the problem was: he was trapped by what he had achieved. He was a very proud man. How was he going to be able to cope with being a mere mortal?

At the end of 1979, when he had been out of work for nearly eighteen months, he was thrown a lifeline of sorts by the chairman of Oxford City, a non-League club in the shadow of its somewhat bigger rival, Oxford United. The job was part-time but Bobby was determined to put everything into it. One good thing was that it gave Bobby the opportunity to link up with Harry Redknapp again. He had rated Harry very highly ever since their days at West Ham, both as a friend and as a potentially top class coach and manager. Harry was entertaining, quick-witted and knowledgeable. Bobby had planned for a long time to invite him to work alongside him as soon as the opportunity came along. 'Let's have a year there and see how it goes,' he suggested to Harry.

Harry joined him as assistant coach, but they quickly realized the impossibility of making anything of the club. There were few facilities and disappointingly small crowds.

'It wasn't easy,' Harry said. 'I'd sit with him at some bleak places in the middle of winter, with about eighty people watching. Nobody could have made a success of that job. It would be pouring with rain, freezing cold, and I'd look at Bobby and think, "It's bad enough for me, but what's the captain of England doing here?" He deserved better. Why wasn't he being given the opportunity to get involved in something worthwhile in football? Think of the knowledge he could have given the kids. He should have been allowed to write his own job description at West Ham.'

The Oxford City job was the nadir for Bobby. Under the terms of his contract, he was obliged to make appearances at various stores around the city. He hated that. Even so, he soldiered on for a year. Then he and the chairman mutually called it quits. It was to be his last job in English management for three years.

Towards the end of his time at Oxford, he started feeling eaten up with defeat. He hated the thought that people knew he was having a tough time. He was proud. It was very difficult for him, having been such a celebrated and public figure for so long, to have fallen from grace so far. I think that in those awful years Bobby died slowly, the golden Bobby that we all worshipped and wanted him to be.

Things didn't work out for him. If he'd put Oxford City onto a winning streak, touched them with a bit of his magic and taken them into the League, it would have been different. But that didn't happen. The failure sapped him. He felt impotent, not knowing how to reverse the tide of bad fortune. With hindsight, I can see that he was showing many of the classic symptoms of depression. I wanted to protect him. He turned to me for support and we still had a very loving marriage, but he felt so humiliated.

When Geoff Hurst ran into big financial problems, he went out and sold insurance. That was admirable, and so in keeping with Geoff, but Bobby was a very different character. I know he would have found it very tough. He was quiet and reserved. He had a shell around him and being the proud man he was, he would have found it difficult to stand on people's doorsteps presenting a sales pitch to amazed potential clients, their mouths gaping open at the sight of the former captain of England trying to sell them life insurance.

How that would have demoralized him. He knew how people perceived him. To them he was a king, a lion. I had seen it for myself. When Fulham got to Wembley in 1975, I watched people calling out his name and lifting up their babies for him to touch. There was real reverence in their eyes.

CHAPTER FOURTEEN

Lost in Translation

Between 1980 and 1981 we soldiered on somehow while I prayed that things would get better, and it really did seem like a godsend when Bobby landed a role in the film *Escape To Victory*. Directed by John Huston, this had a rather ludicrous storyline which involved a group of World War II prisoners using a football match against their German guards to make their bid for freedom. The stars were Michael Caine and Sylvester Stallone.

Just how implausible the whole thing was can be deduced from the fact that Sylvester, Sly to his friends and the would-be keeper, wanted a trampoline put in the goalmouth so that he could soar every time he went to catch the ball. While everybody else's army uniforms were the standard one-size-fits-all issue, Sly's were tailor-made to fit every muscle. One night we were smuggled into Sly's apartment by his PA. It was full of weights.

For Bobby, filming on location in Hungary was just like

old times with West Ham and England. The only difference was that he didn't have Ron Greenwood or Alf Ramsey to answer to. The trip was filled with all the camaraderie and sense of boys playing that Bobby had missed. The gorgeous and mischievous Russell Osman was one of the real footballers who took part in the film, as was Mike Summerbee, another scamp. We stayed at the historic Gellert Hotel, which featured underground steam baths where enormous women scrubbed at guests and flung buckets of cold water over them.

Shakira Caine came along to the filming with Michael. She was stunning, with beautiful liquid eyes like Bambi. I was eager to know the secret of her huge, long eyelashes and asked what mascara she used. She told me the make, which I rushed out to buy, but in spite of spending hours applying the stuff, I never managed to achieve those Bambi eyes myself.

Michael was lovely – a playful personality. One night when all the gang went out to dinner, he started hunting among the flowers on the table. This was at the start of the Eighties, when Hungary was still part of the Eastern bloc, and Michael claimed he was looking for concealed microphones in case the restaurant was bugged.

He also bore what I thought, after a certain amount of wine, was a marked resemblance to Bobby.

'I can't see it,' he said, when I informed him of this.

'Take your glasses off,' I said.

Michael obliged and I scrutinized his face. 'You're right,' I said. 'You don't. Bobby's better-looking.'

'Bloody cheek,' grinned Michael.

Just in case Michael hadn't had enough of the Moores, Bobby also made him the victim of one of his pranks. When the time came to shoot the big match that was the denouement of the film, Michael had to lead his side of prisoners out. He was carrying a few extra pounds and wearing improbably tight shorts and a constraining T-shirt. Ball under one arm, he strutted onto the pitch, declaiming his come-on-lads-we're-gonna-thrash-'em speech to his team-mates. Bobby, of course, had whispered to the lads to hold back, so when Michael finished his call to arms and turned round, he discovered he had been giving this rousing team talk to himself.

It was a funny, funny trip but unfortunately all too short. Back in England after filming had finished, our problems hadn't gone away. They went on through the summer of 1981. Finally, one night, Bobby said, 'What are you going to do about your birthday?'

'I don't know,' I said. 'That's something you usually look after.'

Bobby shrugged. 'You'd better arrange something.'

That was totally out of character. So was the way he raised the subject – after arriving home late and drunk.

My birthday had always been the excuse for Bobby to

organize a major event. He was a romantic and he adored getting the presentation of things just right, so he made a huge fuss about anything like that. He didn't have to have the excuse of a birthday. Valentine's Day would allow full rein to his creativity. So would Mother's Day, and anniversaries of events that were personal to us. He liked springing surprises. From when we were teenagers on our earliest dates, he had gone out of his way to find all his loved ones unique, special presents. When Roberta was six, she had come home one day from school to find Bobby waiting for her in the hall. 'There's something funny about your room,' he told her. 'I think you'd better go and see what it is.'

Roberta dashed upstairs and flung open the bedroom door. On the bed was a white Persian kitten. She christened it Bubbles. All our cats had football names. Bubbles owed his to the West Ham anthem, 'I'm Forever Blowing Bubbles'.

On another occasion, Bobby suggested it was time I had a new car. 'Let's go and look around the showroom to see if there's anything that catches your eye,' he said.

When we arrived at the showroom, the first thing I saw was a Mini Cooper S, in the lovely purplish black colour of an aubergine, with black tinted windows and a huge bow tied round the bonnet. It was mine.

When I remembered funny, thoughtful gestures like that, I felt more concerned than ever at Bobby's offhand attitude. By now I was beginning to be desperately worried about his state of mind.

We did celebrate my birthday in the end, with a party at Morlands. It was a really good one with our close friends, but we used to have lots of parties at Morlands. There was no extra effort put into this occasion, no grand gesture. It was thrown together. I don't even remember what he gave me – I must have been too stunned by his indifference to take it in.

Even then I was able to justify his moody, withdrawn state to myself. The Oxford City job had come to an end and nothing new had come his way. His frustration was obvious. I knew he was in the middle of a personal crisis, depressed and feeling rejected. That was how I explained away his attitude, anyway. I assumed it was not directed at me. With hindsight, I realize that he had been doing things slightly out of character for some months. He was working the after-dinner speech circuit with Kenny Lynch, Rodney Marsh and George Best and would sometimes not come home at night but say he was staying at Kenny's. So maybe something got 'lost in translation' – or maybe, like they say, there are signs you don't want to see, so you don't see them. Maybe Bobby was just a brilliant liar. But the idea that he might have another woman never entered my mind. Not until a few weeks later, when I went out to Marbella with my friend Carly.

Bobby and I had known Carly and her husband, who

both worked in television, since the days of the Mexico World Cup. Bobby often went out with them when he was up in London and he saw more of them than I did. Even so, the four of us often went on shared trips and I thought of her as a fairly close friend who was a lot of fun.

I was off to Marbella because I was looking for an apartment to buy. Despite what everyone had said about Morlands being a disaster for us, the only money we had ever made was on property. We had let go the place in Marbella we had shared with Freddie Harrison to cover some of our debts on Woolston Hall, but we'd always hoped we would be able to find somewhere else one day. Now, thanks to *Escape To Victory*, we had some spare cash to invest.

Once I had found an apartment I liked, I called Bobby to tell him about it. As usual, he was happy for me to make the decision whether to buy it or not, but one thing about his response struck me as odd. 'Put it solely in my name,' he instructed.

Everything else we had was shared. It disturbed me. Because I felt so concerned, I confided my anxieties to Carly. 'Bobby's a wonderful husband,' I said carefully, 'but he's acting quite strangely at the moment.'

'Tina,' said Carly, 'Bobby is having an affair.'

'WHAT?' I reeled back and sank into a chair. 'What are you talking about? I just don't believe it!'

'We ran into him in Tramp,' said Carly. 'He was with another woman.'

I was so stunned I could hardly speak. In the end, I managed to choke out a few words. 'Why are you telling me this?' I said.

'Bobby wanted me to,' she said.

Suddenly, everything seemed unreal. I forgot about buying the apartment. What was happening between me and Bobby was the only thing on my mind.

Mentally, I replayed some of the events of the preceding weeks. I recalled the way he had encouraged me to make the trip to Marbella. The dates had clashed with the wedding of a friend's daughter and I'd wanted to postpone the trip so we wouldn't miss it, but Bobby wouldn't hear of it. 'If you give the wedding a miss, we won't have to buy them a present,' he said.

At the time, that startled me. It wasn't like Bobby to be cheap. Now I found myself putting a different interpretation on his eagerness to avoid the wedding. 'Perhaps he wanted me out of the way so he could see this woman!' I thought. And perhaps he wanted to keep the apartment in his name because he had calculated that it was better that way if it came down to a divorce and a division of our property.

I was in a state of shock and I think Carly was kicking herself for what she had said. She took me out for what was meant to be a calming drink, but instead the two of us got pie-eyed. Things finished up with Carly half-backtracking.

'Maybe I got it wrong,' she said. 'Maybe he was just in company.'

I had to know. Immediately.

'Bobby, I'm really worried,' I said when I got home. I told him what Carly had said.

Bobby almost exploded. 'It just isn't true. No way am I having an affair. It's all lies.'

'But Carly said you told her to tell me.'

'Tell Carly she's a vicious, vindictive bitch.'

The following Sunday we had a drinks party. Carly and her husband were there and soon the social niceties were scrapped as Bobby laid into her. He categorically denied the affair. Equally emphatically, he denied having asked her to intervene and although I didn't fall out with her irrevocably, my friendship with Carly was severely damaged.

I wouldn't have done what she did. In any case, I was angry with her for having disclosed what I thought was a lie. It was only many years later, when I happened to run into Carly's husband in London one day, that the rift began to heal.

'Bobby asked *me* to ask Carly to do it,' he said.

Bobby isn't here, of course, to confirm that.

It wasn't a case of putting a brave front on it and pretending nothing was wrong. As far as I was concerned, nothing *was* wrong. I totally believed what Bobby had said, especially after I challenged him about wanting to put that flat in his name.

'If you want the flat, buy it,' he said. 'Put it in your name. I just want you to believe me. There is no other woman.'

I was completely convinced by him. After all, Bobby had never been a womanizer. I also felt that my job was to encourage him to keep going and lift his spirits in whatever way I could. He was still in that odd remote, morose mood and what I didn't want was for him to take on another hopeless cause like the one he'd left at Oxford City.

Over the year that followed, it became clear that football had all but abandoned him. In summer 1982, a New Zealand company for whom Bobby had done some promotional work invited us to go with them to Spain for the World Cup. We found out that the opening ceremony was going to feature a parade of past champions. The FA hadn't even contacted Bobby, let alone invited him to lead England out. That job had gone to Bobby Charlton.

I was aghast. I can't begin to imagine how Bobby felt. Everything he had done for his country seemed to have been brushed under the carpet.

One day during the tournament, he happened to bump into Ted Croker, general secretary of the FA at the time. 'You must come over and see the lads,' enthused Ted. 'Pop into the dressing room and they'll give you some tickets.'

'Sod that,' said Bobby. 'No way. I'll buy 'em.'

He was really, really angry. To tell the former captain of England to drop by and cadge tickets, when he should have been at the heart of everything to do with England by right, was just insulting. But he was choked about it, too. He was already isolated from League football, but now it was obvious that England had turned their backs on Bobby as well.

I couldn't believe they could do this to the man. I felt like storming up to them and saying, 'What has he *done?*' I wish I had done just that. Perhaps they could have given me a straight explanation. Then I would know what to say to all the people who still ask me why Bobby was rejected by the football establishment. But I can only speculate like everyone else.

My own feeling is that Bobby was too much his own man for their liking. English football was still run by the old boy network and they probably expected a certain deference which he was unable to give. In the early years of his England captaincy, it was hard for him to get his head around the way some of the International Committee addressed him as Ron, because they thought he was Ron Flowers of Wolves, who also happened to have fair hair and play at wing half. Bobby never quite shook off his contempt at the Men In Blazers and although he was never anything but polite, he couldn't suck up to them.

Yet with his presence and his style, he could have been a huge asset to English football as an ambassador. With his

215

knowledge and his ability to relate to youngsters, he would have done marvellous work with the youth team. He wasn't a yes man, he didn't shake the right hands and he wasn't their type, but nothing excuses their failure to use him imaginatively. I strongly believe that Bobby, more than any other England footballer of his era, was a victim of Tall Poppy Syndrome. They were jealous and they wanted to cut him down.

I think Bobby felt guilty about my last birthday being such a low key performance, because later that summer when the date fell due again, he whisked me off on a round-the-world trip. It took us to LA via Perth, where he had a stint of promotional work.

His mood hadn't lifted by the time we got to Perth and the atmosphere between us was quite strained. He left me to sunbathe and shop while he sang for our supper, but I quickly thought, 'To hell with this' and headed off to the hotel bar for a drink.

In those days, incredibly, Men Only bars were still a feature down under and when I sashayed in, the place was packed with males. Heads turned. To be honest, I got a buzz from the attention. By the time Bobby came back I was centre stage, the toast of Perth.

He was taken aback, and secretly I was glad. I'd wanted a reaction from him. I needed to know he still cared.

Leaving my triumphs in Perth behind, we headed on to

LA. It was my first time there, and the fulfilment of a dream – I'd longed to see it for ages.

'I want to take you there in style,' Bobby had said, and he kept his promise. We were booked into the Bel Air and the first morning started with breakfast in bed. That consisted of champagne and strawberries and the present of some beautiful and exotic lingerie.

For lunch Bobby took me to the Dome restaurant, where I had just sat down when a very beautiful black woman said, 'Excuse me.' My mouth fell open. It was Donna Summer, one of Bobby's favourite singers. More to the point, I had sat on her hat.

Donna took it with good humour, and after that things took on an almost dream-like quality as a man with a shaved head strolled up to our table and said, 'Hello, Bobby.' It was Albert Finney. He joined us for lunch and rang the next day with an invitation to escort us round the studio where he was filming.

Later on during the trip, Bobby and I went to visit the world famous Pebble Beach golf and beach resort. As soon as we parked the car and got out, people rushed forward.

'How strange,' I said. 'They even know you here and it's not as if it's a football-loving country.'

'I don't think it's me they're after,' said Bobby, as they passed him by and surrounded me.

We discovered that Abba were expected to arrive that

217

day, and I had been mistaken for Agnetha. If only. Bobby was a huge fan. But we did have a laugh, and I can safely say that it was the first and only time Bobby took second billing to me.

During the trip we took ourselves off to San Francisco as well. That was also fantastic. Bobby couldn't have been nicer or more cheerful. I began to hope that he had come to terms with his problems and that we could move into a new phase at last.

It was ironic that while Bobby was struggling to find a sense of purpose, things were taking off for me in a really fulfilling way.

Roberta and Dean were growing up fast and I'd decided to expand my limited life. I'd tried golf, ladies' lunches and good works – all the traditional ways in which middle class housewives filled their time in those days. After a while I'd started longing for something more challenging. In the long term I hoped it would lead to a bit of financial independence, too.

One of the jobs I had been doing was an assistant to a probation officer, a lovely man called Roy. Roy was a very kind, caring soul with the stereotypical social worker's green cords, rubber-soled shoes and beard. One of my tasks was to visit a man on probation for theft – he was a great character, but I laughed inwardly when he said he had a TV he could let me have on the cheap.

218

Perhaps I might have been reunited with the one that went walkabout from Morlands.

That was one of the more light-hearted cases. Another was really harrowing. It involved a woman charged with murdering her child, who had suffered from cystic fibrosis. I oversaw her visits to her younger child and was part of her support system during her trial at the Old Bailey. She was acquitted, but committed suicide soon afterwards. In spite of the awful sadness of cases like that, it was the kind of work I got a lot out of, and later Roy suggested I should train as a social worker myself. In the end I decided against it, feeling that after all the years it would take me to qualify I would be too old. I wish I had been more confident. It's a decision I've always regretted.

At the same time, I was also working for the Samaritans, the organization that cares for the suicidal. A few years previously, I had seen a TV documentary about their work and the memory stayed with me. I knew how lucky I was. I had an incredible lifestyle thanks to football, and I wanted to give back. So I applied to become a Samaritan and was delighted when they accepted me onto their training course.

Not many people knew I was a 'Sam'. It was the same for everyone who worked there. The attitude was that you could never tell who might feel in need of a Samaritan to talk to. Despair and suicidal thoughts strike at people in all walks of life – people you might know. If someone who was aware you were a Samaritan was with you whooping it up at a party, then they'd think twice about calling the organization in case it was you at the other end of the phone line.

The Samaritans are a wonderful, really supportive organization, not only for the people who use it but also for its volunteers. Once I'd found my feet, I started doing two daytime shifts a week and one overnight shift a month. I made some wonderful friends there. I didn't consider myself a Lady Bountiful and I wasn't playing at it. This was for real. And little did I know what help they would give me in due course, or that what I learnt with the Samaritans would lead me to the full time job I eventually needed to keep myself sane and solvent.

Yes, it was definitely for real. But so, despite the dream trip to LA, were my marriage problems.

CHAPTER FIFTEEN

Who Was That Woman?

Since the collapse of the Oxford City job, Bobby had a lot of spare time on his hands and he took up the many offers of trips and work abroad that came his way. When Roberta and Dean had been younger, I had been able to leave them with Doss while I went with him. Now they were teenagers, they were too much for her and I opted out of Bobby's travels to stay with them at home.

In 1983 he was sounded out about becoming coach to Eastern Athletic, a club in Hong Kong. He went out there to talk to the owner, and from there he was due to fly out to Australia for some short-term coaching work.

Dearest Tina, Roberta and Dean [he wrote from Sydney on 3 September],
Have just returned from Brisbane, where we have been for the last couple of days . . . I am now firmly ensconced in my little family bedroom, with clothes literally scattered in every direction all over the floor as there just

isn't a drawer to be sighted. To be truthful, I wasn't exactly prepared for this. It was described as a penthouse apartment overlooking a sporting complex, but really is a three-bedroomed apartment housing a family of four, that is also used as the company offices and meeting place for all the kids in the clinics (and I think at times some even sleep in at no extra cost!). You can imagine the phone never stops ringing, the front door is continually open, and the stream of bodies seems to go on forever, but as they say here in Australia, 'Good on yer, blue!' . . . Roberta certainly did very well in her exam results, she must be absolutely delighted, so don't forget to say well done for me and to congratulate her. How's Dean getting on with his maths, or has he proceeded to make his teacher a quivering wreck already? You certainly seem to be having fun at Harrods, and I must admit that you and Rita make a super team, so easy to handle and most co-operative!!!

Have spoken to the lawyer in Hong Kong again today regarding the contract, and have told him to make certain that the apartment I have seen is actually made part of the contract. Actually, the more I think about it, the more I think you will love it. The views are really outstanding and the decoration is really very nice and easily acceptable. Young, bright and airy (not at all like me!!!).

Anyway, darling, must start to close now, but before I

do I have enclosed the breakdown of expenses for running the house (frightening, isn't it!), so until I speak to you again take care, God bless and lots of love to you all. Looking forward to seeing you very soon and lots of kisses to you all.
  Love always,
  Bobby XXXXXX

The breakdown of expenses for running Morlands was as daunting as he had said. The mortgage alone was £3,000 a year – huge for the early Eighties. In all, it cost £6,250 a year to keep the house going – approximately £125 a week. The plan was for us to rent it out for six months, the length of Bobby's initial contract with Eastern. After that, we would make a decision about extending the rental based on whether the job was working out.

A few days later, I had a call from the agent in Hong Kong. The negotiations about the apartment being part of the contract had been successful. What was more, the apartment Bobby had set his heart on for me was still available. But we had to let the agent know within twenty-four hours if we wanted it.

A friend and colleague in the Samaritans, Chris, was with me when the call about the flat came through. That was lucky, because I was thrown into a panic. I felt Bobby had to be the one to take the decision on the apartment, but it was already late at night in Australia. On the other hand, if I left calling him until the morning I might miss him if he went off to work early.

I decided to make the call then and there. First I got the city code wrong and found myself speaking to someone in Melbourne. Then, on my next try, the phone was answered by a sleepy female voice. I thought I'd got through to yet another wrong number but said, 'Can I speak to Bobby Moore?'

'Who are you?' she said.

'I'm Bobby's wife. I want to speak to him.'

'One moment,' she said, yawning.

Seconds later, an even more sleepy Bobby came to the phone.

'The flat's available,' I said. 'Perhaps you should inform whoever that was.' Then I put the receiver down. I felt sick and my knees were weak. I turned to Chris but found I couldn't speak.

She looked at me. 'Tina, are you all right?'

I shook my head. I couldn't get my breath. Then, as she reached out to me, I gasped, 'Chris, I can't believe it. A woman answered the phone. A *woman*. I think he's with her. I mean, with her. *In bed with her.*'

At that point, Bobby rang back in a panic but I cut him short. 'Who *was* that woman?' I demanded.

'It's the sister of the man who owns the flat.'

'I don't believe you,' I said, and hung up.

He rang back three more times but I just kept on saying

it. I was absolutely beside myself with shock and disbelief. *The sister of the man who owned the flat.* How could he try and fob me off with that? It felt so wrong!

The next day he rang again. 'I'm coming home right away,' he said.

I was still hot with fury on the outside, cold with fear underneath. The only thing I could do was go through the motions and wait until I saw him again.

'Bobby Moore . . .'
  'Bobby Moore . . .'
  'That's Bobby Moore . . .'

The whispers ricocheted around Harrods ground floor as he strolled towards the make-up department. Even after a 24-hour flight and a taxi ride into Knightsbridge straight from the airport, he looked immaculate and absolutely gorgeous. As usual, the scene was like the parting of the waves. Out of the corner of my eye I could see the women stand aside to let him pass, their eyes following him speculatively.

I could tell he was apprehensive because he kept his head down as he walked through the displays of lotions and potions towards me. I wasn't too happy, either. In fact, I was aghast. I hadn't expected him to turn up in Harrods. I hadn't been working there long. I'd taken a job there selling make-up, fitting it in alongside my work with Samaritans. It was to give me that small amount of financial independence I'd been looking for in the hope that it could help Bobby's money problems a little.

There was one hitch. No one at the store knew I was married to him. If it had gone round that I was Mrs Bobby Moore, it would have been a matter of hours before headlines appeared in the papers saying that we were absolutely broke and that I'd been forced to go out to work to save the family fortunes.

I have no idea how we got home. My mind had frozen. I was just so frightened and my sixth sense was telling me that something was seriously wrong. There was something different about him. He couldn't look me in the eye. I was very curt and chilly. I was trying to punish him, even though he kept denying that anything was wrong. 'I'm telling you the truth,' he insisted. 'The girl who answered the phone was who I said she was.'

He kept trying to win me over, and at night he would cuddle me and try to make me receptive to him. I pulled away. I wanted him to suffer the way I had. Then after a few nights of clinging to the side of the bed, I decided this was ludicrous and turned to him. Only for him to act cold.

It was time we stopped this ridiculous play-acting and got to the point. 'Look,' I said. 'What's really going on here?'

'I think I've got a bit of a problem,' he said.

'You – think – you've – got – a – bit – of – a – *problem*.'

'Tina, it's not you. It's nothing to do with you.'

'What is it to do with, then? Was that someone you're seeing who answered the phone? Were you lying to me?'

'No, of course not. Please, Tina, I assure you, it's nothing I can't work out. I love you more than anything in the world. You and the children *are* my world. It's just that everything in my life is in such a mess. I'm worried about money, I'm worried about the mortgage, I'm worried about not having a settled job.'

'We'll sell the house, then. I hate you being like this.'

'But you love the house,' he said. 'So do I. It's our dream home. I promise you things will get better.'

With excruciating timing, we were scheduled to go out on an all-expenses visit to Bermuda on the *QE2*, one of the perks that Bobby was still offered. The trip was organized by Pye, then a big name in radio and television manufacturing. As luck would have it, just before we were due to leave, I bent to get something from a bottom drawer and my back went into spasm. Typical – things always happen to me! I was in such pain I had to be pushed onto the boat in a wheelchair. It was a classic case of Sod's Law – I'd bought a lot of exotic lingerie to win and woo Bobby all over again, but for the first few days I could hardly walk. Anything more exciting than that was completely out of the question.

Once aboard the *QE2*, Bobby saw to it that we were looked after in style. Before the start of the cruise he tipped the waiter, who repaid us for the largesse by giving us mounds of caviar the size of motorcycle helmets, much to everyone else's disappointment – they only got a couple of teaspoonfuls, even our hosts. The waiter was very camp and loved it when Bobby teased him – he'd fallen for Bobby in a big way.

Bermuda was one of Bobby's favourite places and one he had always promised to take me to one day. It should have been a memorable, romantic trip, but there was a terrible atmosphere between us. The weather wasn't that good, either. After my bad back had eased, we hired a motor scooter to tour the island and on one of our excursions he had to pull up so sharply I nearly slipped off the saddle.

'You're trying to throw me off the bike and kill me!' I said, which made him laugh and relaxed the tension between us. But we really had a tough time.

After days of silence on the only subject that really mattered, I finally forced him to talk about it again. 'Look, Bobby, I'm a counsellor,' I said. 'I deal with these things all the time. You're torturing me. It's the not knowing that really kills you.'

It was the same story. 'I've got a problem and I'm trying to solve it.'

But I persisted. 'Have you met somebody?'

'I have,' he said, 'but I don't know where I am.'

'What's her name? How long has it been going on?'

'Doesn't matter.'

Who Was That Woman?

My gut feelings had been right. I was devastated. He refused to tell me anything about her, even her name, but I could sense he was still vacillating between the two of us and I was determined to do everything I could to win him back.

Perhaps because he realized he'd been so rotten to me, he suggested staying on in Bermuda an extra two days. That simply prolonged the agony. He was so preoccupied that I even beat him at golf.

When we flew back to London, we dropped into Harvey Nichols before heading for Morlands. We'd wanted to see how Roberta was getting on, because she had a holiday job there, but all we achieved was inflicting our tensions on her. The atmosphere between Bobby and me was so icy we could have chilled champagne in it, except that champagne was the last thing we felt like. I could still get nothing from him beyond the fact that he had 'met someone' and he didn't know where he was at. I found him so impossible to get through to that I began to sympathize with Ron Greenwood. Now I knew what it felt like to be on the wrong side of Bobby's emotional blockades.

It was almost a relief when he set off for Hong Kong to start work, but I felt at a loss about what to do. Bobby still expected me to follow him out there and set up home. 'Let's carry on with our plans,' he said. 'We'll get through this.'

I re-read the letter he had sent from Australia over and

229

over again. The handwriting, as always, was beautiful. The tone was warm and affectionate. Perhaps I was in denial, but it didn't seem to me like a letter from a man who had another woman.

I made arrangements for Roberta and Dean. Roberta was going to stay with friends and Dean became a temporary boarder at his school, Forest. The plan was for them to come out to Hong Kong once the holidays started. Then I approached a letting agency, which found me an American who wanted to take Morlands for six months.

At the last minute, I changed my mind and opted out of going ahead with the rental. While I believed that Bobby, like me, really wanted to give our marriage a chance, I had some misgivings about how Hong Kong would work out. I felt it was too much of a risk to leave myself without a bolthole if things were as bad as they had been in Bermuda.

Even so, when the time came for me to join him there, I took practically everything I possessed. I wasn't going there on holiday. I was going there to live with my husband. For the length of his contract with Eastern. At his suggestion.

At Kai Tak airport my mounds of luggage and I were met by a very, very aloof Bobby. That night we went out with Alan and Lesley Ball to one of the clubs catering for the expat community. Alan was Bobby's second-in-command at Eastern. Probably of all the people he went around with – and certainly of all his 1966 World Cup team-mates – Alan was closest to him. Bobby never confided in anyone,

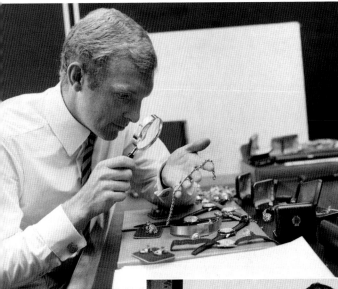

Left: Not *the* bracelet. Bobby at the Hatton Gardens office of Bobby Moore Jewellery Ltd.

Right: Bobby looking surprisingly happy with life, with Jimmy Greaves and an admiring fan, after his detention in Bogota, 1970.

Left: Under arrest! I arrive in Guadalajara . . . with a special escort to clear customs.

Above: Bobby showing how it should be done – and letting his football do the talking for him.

Above: Proud day. Bobby receiving his OBE in 1967 for services to football.

Left: Alf Ramsey with his 'lieutenant on the pitch'.

Sand dance. Entertaining the locals on Copacabana beach.

Almost bosom pals . . . Bobby and Pele warming up for Team America against an England XI.

Above: Getting in too deep. Overseeing the building of the Woolston Hall swimming pool.

Right: Chilling out. Bobby at ease during an England training session.

Below: Go West Young Man. Bobby played for San Antonio Thunder in the American NASL in the summer of 1976.

The loves of my life: (from top left, clockwise) Roberta, Dean and Poppy, Ava and Freddie.

Above: Family reunion. Bobby's return from Bermuda, Heathrow airport, 1971.

Left and above: Bobby's back. Returning to his stage for the FA Cup Final, Fulham v West Ham, May 1975 and arriving in London for the big match.

Below: Acapulco, 1970, Bobbyand Geoff drowning their disappointment after England's World Cup exit.

Left: Father and son. Forget the England caps, this was Bobby's favourite.

Below: Off the deep end in Marbella. Most people didn't know what a practical joker Bobby could be.

Above: Long or short? Bobby in indecisive mode, on holiday in Portugal.

Above: Mixed memories. Our last holiday as a family together, in our apartment in Hong Kong in 1983.

Left: Honouring President Bill Clinton, the Irish American of the Year, at the Plaza Hotel in New York.

Right: With my cousin Jenny at Roberta's wedding, October 1995, outside St Paul's Cathedral.

Left: Tina Moore in 2005. Bobby won 108 caps. I only had one.

but there was a huge amount of liking, respect and even fondness between the two of them.

I liked Alan's wife, Lesley, very much, too. She was a strong, good-looking, vibrant, laughing girl with lovely blonde hair and lots of personality, every bit a match for her fiery, larger-than-life husband. Their daughters had been to prep school with Roberta and because there had been no boys in the Ball household at the time, Alan adored Dean and treated him as an honorary son.

The night out with the Balls was the first of many disasters. Bobby got really, really drunk. Then he casually announced that he was due to go off to a match the next day. 'On my own,' he said.

'Can't I go?' I asked.

'No.'

'Can't you put me first in your life instead of second to football for once?'

Bobby said, 'What makes you think you're as high up as second?'

I hit him with my bag. 'I'm going home!' It was an instant reaction to his rudeness. I was so angry and upset at having been treated so cruelly. I wasn't used to being talked to in such a callous way. It was totally out of character, and especially embarrassing for it to happen in front of Lesley and Alan. They just didn't know where to put their faces as I walked out.

The next day Bobby went off to the match. When he

231

came back in the evening, he poured himself a drink and said, 'I've got a major problem. I really like this person.'

'You what?' I yelled. 'You really like this person?' I was utterly bewildered by then. I thought I was going mad. 'You've dragged me two-thirds of the way round the world to be with you and now you're telling me you like someone else! If that's the case, just get my plane tickets, cancel the kids' tickets. I'm going back to England.'

He just looked at me and didn't move.

'I mean it,' I said. 'If this is the way you feel, I'm not staying here. Being treated in this awful, icy manner. After having come so far to be with you.'

'I think I can work through it.'

'THINK you can work through it! I'm going!'

'Tina, I beg you, I will work through it. Give me a chance.'

'But how?' I said. 'What are you going to do? We have children coming over here. It's going to be Christmas soon. I don't want them here in this atmosphere. How are we going to manage?'

Initially, things improved a bit after that. Bobby must have realized I was shattered. This was the first time he had actually admitted that things were serious. He had always denied it before.

'What's her name?' I asked for what felt like the millionth time.

No response.

Who Was That Woman?

'Please, Bobby. Talk to me about it. Help me understand what's happening.'

Then, finally, he said it. 'I'm in love with her.'

I physically collapsed when he told me. I was beside myself with grief. I think it was because he had said the word *love*. That was when true anguish took over. I experienced it as physical pain. I couldn't eat. I'd take sleeping pills, then wake up again within two hours. I lost 20 lb in as many days. My body had gone into shock.

Bobby was suffering, too. He hated himself for what he was doing but couldn't help it. He would pick arguments, walk out and not come back until the next day. He would say he had spent the night on the beach, when actually he had been with her. I had no idea at the time that she had been in Hong Kong part or all of the time. I only found out twenty years later, when I read about it in an article she had written.

Bobby was having a bad time at Eastern. It was such a different culture. We used to go to matches where people would sit around us eating chicken feet and casting the bones on the floor. The team wasn't winning. The Chinese owner, who was fabulously wealthy, wanted immediate success with his toy and insisted on being hands-on involved. I don't think Bobby was able to give it 100%. With his girlfriend also in Hong Kong he was being torn three ways, between her and me and the job.

He was leading a hectic double life, trying to kick-start a second career that refused to get moving. He was fundamentally a decent man. I don't think he could deal with all the deception and guilt, and that affected the way he dealt with the challenges of management. And because that didn't go well for him, his confidence was sapped again. Again and, this time, totally.

I loved Bobby so much. I didn't want to lose him. I begged, cajoled, lost all my dignity. I'd have done anything at that point. You just cave in. I was in this alien place, not knowing what was going to happen.

Bobby didn't want me to discuss our problems with anyone back in England. I thought, 'To hell with that,' and put a call through to Samaritan Chris, as she'd been in on the drama from the very beginning. I got Bobby on the line to her, but she didn't get any further with him than I had.

Afterwards, she said to me, 'Tina, he wouldn't discuss anything with me. He closed up – just shut me out.'

'Frustrating, isn't it?' I said. 'That's how he is all the time with me now.'

I was trying to be calm, but inside I was despairing. Everything was pretty horrendous, but what I really couldn't cope with was the fact that he wouldn't talk. At one point, I even rang the Hong Kong branch of Samaritans.

I reached my lowest point on a bus, sobbing out my story to a Chinese woman. It was unreal. I was madly in love with Bobby still. He was my one and only man and had been since I was a teenager. Not only that – he was my best friend. I thought my world had ended. I was frightened. Terrified.

Fool that I was, I thought that once the children arrived for Christmas and we were a family unit again, things might get back to somewhere near normal. Christmas had always been a special time for us, with lots of fun and presents and parties. But this one was diabolical, right from the evening when Roberta went out on a date with someone who was a real football fan. He was desperate to meet Bobby. After Dean went to bed, she and I sat up with him, waiting, but Bobby never came home that night. How humiliating.

The Balls must have been aware of something going on. Annie and Billy Semple, who were also in Hong Kong, had seen Bobby with his girlfriend and news got around fast. The Balls were a fantastic couple and Alan was a great family man. I don't think he would have liked what was happening. As for me, I must have driven Lesley mad, going over and over what was happening. It was an awkward situation for her but she was a really supportive friend.

One day before Christmas, the team and their families went on a trip on a junk to Lamma Island and I sobbed to Lesley all the way. We had lunch at a seafood restaurant in one of its two villages, Yung Shu Wah, where a famous hippie colony was situated.

When I wanted to go to the loo, I was directed to the first floor of the restaurant, where I turned left instead of right and burst into a room filled with chanting monks in orange robes. One of them explained that they were weaning a man off drugs. Soon I was weeping and wailing even louder than them as I told them what a terrible time I was having. Two of them escorted me from the loo back to Bobby. They told him they would pray for us, and started chanting while I sat on his lap. Everyone was falling about laughing. Bobby raised his eyes heavenwards (rather appropriately) and said drily, 'Only my wife would come back from the Ladies with two monks.'

At least I could still make him laugh.

Roberta was nearly eighteen and in her A Level year, while Dean was approaching fourteen. As soon as they joined us, they became aware of the problems. Like me, they had no idea that the problem had a name, Stephanie, but they could see their parents' marriage falling apart and it was hard for them at the ages they were. On Christmas Eve, we gave a dinner party in the apartment for the entire team. Bobby kept sniping at me. He would realize how awful he sounded and be apologetic and loving but then the sarcasm and insults would start again. The children weren't used to us being at loggerheads and Dean locked himself in his bedroom, absolutely choked. Lesley Ball had to climb through a window to get to him and console him.

There was a terrible atmosphere between Bobby and Alan. Bobby was drunk yet again and Alan had had a few as well by then and got very upset with him. Ostensibly, the argument was about football because the team weren't winning, but there was a subtext, with a lot of stuff insinuated about Bobby's other problem. It turned into a hammer-and-tongs verbal, with Alan *screaming* at Bobby – at one point I thought they were going to come to blows. In fact, it ended up with Bobby and Alan falling into each others arms, bear hugging and making up.

On Christmas Day, we tried to act like any other family. Bobby gave me a watch, a Jaeger-le-Coultre. It had been a favourite make of my mother's, so perhaps he had taken a lot of care choosing it. I gave him a watch, too – a Cartier. He was very nice to us all that day and I was praying that we might be able to resolve things somehow, but soon afterwards he started wearing a different watch. He said it had been given to him by a club supporter.

In a situation like ours, you become ultra-sensitive to the point of obsession. I thought that the new watch must have been a Christmas present from his girlfriend. Or perhaps he just couldn't bring himself to wear my gift to him.

One night we went to a club opening. It was called Rumours – how appropriate. Annie and Billy Semple were running it. I was so thin by then that the suit I had brought out with me from England was hanging off me. I was frail and couldn't eat. For some reason, when we were leaving the club my attention was caught by a young woman. She said, 'Goodnight' and Bobby said, 'Goodnight' back to her.

I thought, *That's her.*

As I've said, I hadn't a clue at the time that Stephanie was in Hong Kong during some of that period. I had, of course, plagued Bobby, asking him countless times if she was, but he had always categorically denied it and I had believed him. Old habits die hard, I suppose. But my feeling that night was overwhelmingly strong. I have no idea who it might have been, but I started obsessing that she might have seen me while I was unawares. Even thinking about it made me feel violated.

The next day, we went to the beach at Repulse Bay. Bobby swam out to a raft straightaway. I swam out after him and found him sitting on the raft, crying. I tried to comfort him. Of course, with hindsight I realize he needed to be on his own and I should have let him be, but at the time I just couldn't bear to leave him like that. I just wanted to drink him in. I knew we were breaking up. I was desperate to make it right.

He started swimming back to the beach, probably to get away from me. No such luck. As my mother always said, Tina's a strong swimmer. I was alongside him stroke for stroke! As we lay on the beach talking, I drew a big heart in the sand. A butterfly came down and landed on it, and I said, 'Oh Bobby, perhaps it's a sign.' Real Mills and Boon stuff. I was looking for *anything*.

'Bobby, I've got to go.'

It was early in the New Year. The rumours hadn't taken long to get around and the press had started taking an interest in the state of our marriage. I learnt later that what was going on between Bobby and Stephanie had been known to some journalists and players for a long time, and local reporters had been keeping the British press up to date.

Knowing that the press were sniffing around decided me. I had to go back to England with the children. They were suffering, I felt ill, and I think Bobby realized I couldn't go on. He needed some space to work things out, too.

I got absolutely smashed on the flight home, and the press were waiting on the doorstep at Morlands. Head down, I hurried inside, only to hear the phone ringing. It was Bobby. 'Are you all right?' he asked.

I glanced out of the window. The press were still there. Someone was rattling the flap of the letterbox. 'Please,' I said. 'Help me. I can't cope with this.'

'We've got two options,' he said. 'Either you get on a plane and come right back, or I'll come to you.'

'I can't face going back,' I said.

'All right,' he said. 'I'm on my way.'

As soon as I put the phone down, I knew it wasn't a

good idea. I didn't know how I should act or what Bobby was going to be like. Instead of being happy that he was returning to me, I was scared.

I was right to feel the way I did. I knew that as soon as Bobby walked in. He looked really ill and gaunt and went straight to bed. He stayed there for twenty-four hours, just shaking. I lay with my arms around him, trying to warm him, cuddle him, make the marriage work again, but he was like a frightened jack rabbit. Even then, I couldn't accept it was over. Neither of us could deal with the situation.

'You have no idea how to react to this, have you?' he said.

'How could I?' I said. 'I've grown up with you. I've been with you for twenty-five years. You were my best friend as well as my husband and now you're cutting me out of your life.'

He was right. I didn't have any idea how to deal with it at all. I was lost.

CHAPTER SIXTEEN

Not-So-Sweet Carolina

It was the spring of 1984 and I was still clinging to the hope that I could save my marriage. Bobby's six-month contract at Eastern was at an end and he had returned to England. He was out of a football job again and back to doing promotional work.

To be honest, I don't remember much about those weeks. They were too painful. My diary for the time was bald and to the point. 'Bobby gone,' said one entry. Another said, 'Bobby gone again.' He must have been travelling a lot and I must have been trying to put a brave face on it.

I dreaded the times when he was home. The only word I can think of to describe them is 'vile'. We were living on a see-saw and our mood swings were wearying and tiring for each other. I struggled to keep hold of my temper. He was all over the place and cried a lot. At other times he was cutting and said a lot of awful things about me and our marriage that I found very hard to bear.

'How can you say these things?' I asked him desperately.

'I know it's been difficult for the last eighteen months but before that, we had the most incredible marriage and we were incredibly happy. We had tremendous fun together. There was so much love and tenderness there, and we were so close. It wasn't so long ago that you wanted us to have another baby. You were always there for me . . . Our marriage was fine before you met this woman.'

Roberta and Dean coped with it as best they could. They immersed themselves in friends and schoolwork, and as a family we tried to present a united front to the world. Bobby and I went out to dinner with friends and carried on our social life as if everything was normal. But living a lie was strange, and a strain. It seemed like a godsend when Rodney Marsh got in touch. Rodney was in his second year managing at Carolina Lightnin' in Charlotte. He couldn't believe that our England captain was out of work and when he found out, he was on the line straightaway with the offer of a six-month contract as player-coach.

'What are you going to do?' I asked Bobby.

'It's best that I go,' he said curtly.

Even then, though, he seemed to be vacillating. He wrote to me from Carolina on 6 May and although the letter was much cooler than the one he had written from Hong Kong and I was 'Dear Tina' rather than 'Dearest', it was several pages long and, again, not the letter of a man who was planning to leave his wife. Far from it – he was expecting me to fly out to Charlotte to join him.

Not-So-Sweet Carolina

Dear Tina [he wrote],
Many thanks for the mail that I received the day before yesterday, and also the letters that were included from you and the children. I am sorry I have not been able to write earlier, but have been working morning and after-noon about six days of the week, and more often than not Rodney wants to see me after training to go over other matters in the club that he is dealing with when he is not with the team. All in all it's been fairly hectic, and for an old man like me it gets very tiring and quite demanding!

The apartment is more than adequate. Two bedrooms, two bathrooms, and more or less all you need in the kitchen. Obviously the furnishings are very basic, but if you wanted to make the effort and put the personal touches to it, you could make it even better. I haven't done anything about that side at the moment, so it is still much the same as when I arrived! . . .

After two more pages of bland waffle, he finished by saying:

I am glad that everything is OK at home, and you are all keeping well and in good spirits. Give my regards to all and sundry, and I look forward to writing again soon, so until then take care, God bless, and lots of love.
Bobby XXXXXX

I didn't know what to make of that letter. Looking back, it was very much how Bobby was at the time – evasive. It's clear to me now that he was just going through the motions, as if writing to me was a twenty-five-year-old habit he couldn't break. But I don't think that any outsider reading it would have recognized that he was leading a double life.

Soon after, he rang. 'Come over for the summer,' he said. 'Bring the kids. Have a holiday.'

In a way I wanted to go. I love travelling, and the fact that he had asked me to join him gave me hope. I would have kicked myself if I hadn't tried everything.

'It's worth one last shot,' I thought. 'Perhaps we can still turn things around.' So with great trepidation, I packed and headed across the Atlantic to Charlotte. Bobby met me at the airport. As I walked through the concourse with him, I sneaked a glance at him. The problem was still there. I just knew. He was aloof.

Some holiday this was going to be.

At the apartment, there were clues all over the kitchen. In the cupboard under the sink was a huge box of washing powder that a man on his own would never need. Then I found a hunk of parmesan in the fridge and I almost wanted to laugh. Bobby was no Jamie Oliver. The idea of him enjoying a bachelor night at home in his pinny, rustling up pasta penne, just didn't ring true. When he cooked us a dish containing prawns with apples for dinner, I thought to myself, 'God knows where that recipe came from.' I had my suspicions.

We sat up. I was jetlagged and I suppose I was getting pretty smashed. It was the only way of blotting out the pain. Nothing had changed. It was the end of the line. In the end, I had to go to bed. There was nowhere else to sleep. I had to share a bed with him. 'I must have a brandy to get to sleep,' I slurred.

Bobby reached for the bottle, took one look at me, then poured the brandy down the sink.

Even then, I tried to put the most hopeful slant on it. Perhaps he knew I'd wake up with a terrible hangover if I had any more. I tried to tell myself that it meant he still cared.

The next day, I thought, 'I can't do this any more. I know now that there's no way anything can be re-ignited between us.' All the same, I was determined not to have a repeat performance of Hong Kong, with the children once again having to endure our hostility and tension. Specifically, I vowed I wasn't going to lose it in front of them ever again.

So we made the best we could of the circumstances. Bobby spent most of the time training with the team and I played tennis, enjoyed the pool and made some wonderful new friends. The children and I did some fun things. Bobby and I were civil to each other to keep up appearances, but everything was carried out on a very superficial level. There was no warmth between us. It was awful.

One thing Bobby did do was obtain tickets for Roberta and me to see a Marvin Gaye concert. When the two of us arrived, we had a drink in the bar and met the conductor of the band. Another conquest for Roberta. We were invited backstage to meet Marvin in person – what a thrill!

The show was great. Marvin was the sexiest man, strutting around the stage in the tiniest of gold boxer shorts. But after the show Roberta wanted to make a few repairs to hair and make-up and by the time we got backstage, he had gone. He had left a message, though. It said he was sorry he couldn't meet the beautiful English girl but we Brits were too slow and that's why we lost the USA.

Thinking about it, Marvin was right. I was too slow and too trusting to realize what had been going on. That's why I was losing my man.

On most evenings, we had dinner as a family in the apartment. Then I would wash down a sleeping pill (a newly acquired habit) with a couple of glasses of wine and cling on to the edge of the bed.

Then Bobby had a call from England. Would he be interested in managing Southend United? Would he hell!!! Of course he would. It was what he had always wanted. He accepted immediately.

It was hardly big time – the club was in Division Three –

but I was delighted for him. I still cared about him and his career and thought it was great that someone in England had had a change of heart and was offering him the chance to succeed. I wanted him to have a shot at what he'd longed for and had been deprived of. At the same time I was happy at the prospect that he would have to fly back to England to negotiate terms. It would be a relief to be spared the burden of living with someone whose thoughts were elsewhere.

The night after Bobby had gone back, I went out to dinner at a local restaurant with Kelly, one of the new friends I had made. We were sitting at the table when the waiter started chatting to me.

'What are you doing in Charlotte?' he asked.

'I came here to join my husband,' I said. 'He's a footballer, Bobby Moore.'

'But you're not Mrs Moore,' he said. 'She's got dark hair.'

After the waiter had gone, Kelly said. 'Tina, I am so sorry. I wasn't going to say anything. He's right. There was a woman around here with Bobby. She was dark and I think she could be an air hostess. She left just before you arrived.'

I must have looked as sick as I felt. Kelly was appalled. 'You're so lovely,' she said, 'and you've got such a nice family. I can't believe he's got someone else.'

It still came as a total shock when I opened the itemized

phone bill that arrived at the apartment while Bobby was away, but it made sense, as there had been calls made to places all over the world. Bobby had refused to say anything about her at all. All I knew about her had been gleaned from Kelly and the waiter. She was dark and an air hostess.

'You wrote to me and called me lots of times after you came out here,' I said to Bobby when he returned from England, 'and almost every time you asked me to come over with the children. You expected me to set up home here with them. But your friend's been around all along. You've been asking me to pretend everything's all right. You know I can't do that any longer.'

In August, Bobby finished at Charlotte and left to start work at Southend. I stayed to see out the holidays with the children. Friends organized a surprise birthday party for me and Rodney brought some of the team along. He carried on being kind and supportive, although I knew he felt uncomfortable. 'You know, Tina, I like you both,' he said one day over coffee. 'I'm in a very awkward position.'

I was all too aware of that. All of the friends Bobby and I shared would be feeling the same. But I wasn't yet up to thinking about implications of that sort. I was drained. I had nothing left to give. I had put on a brave face for so long that I was actually physically weary. It had been a year of absolute mental torment, of, 'Yes, we'll try and make a go of it'; 'No, it's finished'; 'I think I still love you'; 'Let's see if we can work through it'; 'How can I ever leave you?' Now I knew in my heart it was over.

Even then, Bobby didn't leave completely. He was waiting at Morlands when I came back with the children from Charlotte. 'Please, Tina, shall we try one more time?' he said.

Amazingly, I still loved Bobby deeply, without reservation. 'Yes,' I said.

What a mistake. He might as well have been a lodger. His suitcase was stuffed, ready to go. He kept his shaving gear and toothbrush in his wash case and took it with him every time he wanted to use the bathroom, as if he was at a hotel. Most of the time he sat in his bar to stay out of my way.

After a week of tension and coldness I had had enough. I was fed up of the pretence and the pussyfooting around, and because I was churning inside it was getting harder and harder to control my feelings. It wasn't healthy. Things had to be resolved one way or another. One of us had to take control and it was going to have to be me.

I went to his bar and sat down opposite him. 'Bobby', I asked him, 'does my presence here offend you?'

'Well, yes.'

I looked at him. At that moment, it wasn't that he'd betrayed me with another woman or that he'd lied to me

249

and humiliated me and said some terrible, cruel things. It was the fact that he looked so unbelievably handsome, sitting there in his red tracksuit. 'Even now,' I thought wonderingly, 'you look so cool and collected. How do you manage it?' But this time it wasn't 'What a man!' that I was thinking.

'Bobby, you're killing us all,' I said. 'You have to make a decision. I'm going to go out now and when I come back I want you either to say you're really going to try, or I want you gone.'

I went out. I came back. He was gone.

My instant emotion was relief. I was so thankful that I wouldn't have to live with this misery and uncertainty any longer that I opened a bottle of champagne.

'I fought for him,' I thought. 'I lost. That's it.'

But the next day, reality kicked in. 'My God,' I thought, 'I'm on my own.' I was in pieces.

I went through every emotion. I wrote page after page of letters to Bobby, but never sent any of them. I felt no anger towards his friend, although I didn't admire or respect her. He was, after all, a married man. It was Bobby himself I was angry with, for leaving me and splitting up our family. That wasn't a continuous feeling. Some of the time, I blamed myself. I kept asking myself what I had done, because he was such a wonderful man and I couldn't believe that some-one who had been so loyal and loving could have gone off and left me for nothing. We had been together for such a long time. You can get complacent within a marriage. Had I taken him for granted, or not made enough effort?

At other times, when I felt calmer, I was able to be more rational. No one could ever be totally blameless just as nobody could ever be completely, one hundred per cent, at fault. There was no point hating him or myself. It was circumstances.

We had had tremendous financial trials and tribulations and a huge mortgage to service. Bobby had been used to living life to the full and all of a sudden, the good things were eluding his grasp. I'm convinced it was that period of despair and frustration that led him to look outside our marriage. He was emotionally vulnerable, feeling humiliated and rejected. He badly needed a boost to his ego. Nobody in the football world appeared to value what he had to give.

He probably wanted to be free of all the cares and responsibilities. Towards the end of our marriage he sometimes talked of leading a simpler life. I could understand his longing to opt out, although I wasn't too impressed when in the cause of the simple life he started trying to persuade me to wear jeans, boots and bomber jackets!

Obviously Dean and Roberta had their take on it. They thought that after things didn't work out the way he had hoped in football, he must have felt very lost. Where do you go from there? Perhaps he felt he'd been through his football life with me and now he was going to take a different direction with someone else.

Even then, there were some funny moments. 'You wouldn't let me have a dog,' Bobby claimed at one point. That was one of the reasons, apparently, that he had looked elsewhere. Obviously he had forgotten about the hideous canine I once rescued from the Dogs' Home. It was white with a single black spot over one eye, so inevitably we called it Patch, and it had a high, curly tail so you could see its bottom. Not only did it howl all night but it took an instant and complete aversion to Bobby the minute it saw him, leaping up to bite his arm. It was actually hanging by the teeth and swinging from Bobby's flesh. Never let it be said I prevented Bobby from having a dog.

I had no idea what to do with my life. I got through the days somehow, drinking too much and chain-smoking. I just felt fogged and numb. I was in a daze.

Langan's Brasserie in Mayfair had always been one of our favourite places, and one day he called me and asked to meet for lunch. Like all women spurned, I took special care with what I wore because I wanted to look my best. Bobby was suitably complimentary and while we were eating lunch I happened to notice a friend of mine at the bar. She was talking to a couple of men. Bobby saw her, too. 'Tina,' he said suddenly, 'you're a very good-looking woman. You'll be all right. You'll meet someone.'

'Bobby, you're insulting me,' I said. 'If that's what you really think, you don't know me. I can't switch my emotions off and on at will. How could you think I'd be that shallow? Do you really think I want to sit at bars trying to meet men? You are so wrong.'

He sighed. 'I don't want it to be like this,' he said. 'I'm so sorry I hurt you, but really, you must believe me, I do care about you. I still love you. I'll always be there for you.'

'But you're not there for me, and you can't be,' I said. I knew he liked his life neat and tidy with everything in its own compartment, but this was one compartment I wasn't going to let him put me in.

CHAPTER SEVENTEEN

Brief Encounter

Bobby had been gone more than a year when I started to realize I had to get my act together. Although it was difficult to admit it to myself, I was handling the split badly. I was drinking and smoking too much and still relying on sleeping pills. I had played on the fact that Bobby couldn't steel himself to let go completely, hoping against hope that I could manipulate him into coming back to me, working on the guilt and anguish he felt. I was *hurt*.

I deluged Doss with phone calls. I felt lost and heartbroken and I was worried about the children. Burdening her with my own anger and sadness made me feel guilty, but I didn't know who else I could turn to. Doss was always very patient. She tried to reassure me, but what on earth could she say? She found the split very hard to come to terms with herself. Bobby had been reared to have strong family values. What happened wasn't something she welcomed. No one in her family had ever had a broken marriage.

Even after Bobby left, he rang constantly to find out if I was coping. He couldn't come to terms with what he had done. Leaving his children and splitting up a family was a truly dreadful thing for a man like him. All the values he had grown up with were turned upside down. He didn't like untidiness or ugliness in anything, especially his private life. The split was tough for him as well as for me.

He would drive over to Morlands to see me. The two of us would sit on the terrace, trying to thrash things out. Every time he came, the children would think he was staying, so when he left it was like a new wound for them, but we were too wrapped up in our own pain to realize how much it affected Roberta and Dean. I was so immersed in grief and unhappiness I couldn't take on board how much they were suffering too. I was still there, but I wasn't there – that's the only way I can put it. It was a rotten period which had a tremendous impact on them both. They had always idolized their father and now he had fallen off the pedestal, big time.

Their school work bore the brunt. Roberta, who had notched up 10 O-Levels without difficulty, really had her work cut out to concentrate on her A-Levels although, being a fighter, she ended up acquitting herself extremely well. Dean, at fifteen, felt angry and terribly, terribly rejected. That age can be hard for any boy. Dean was in real pain and it showed in almost everything he did. I was so desperate about Dean's acting up that in desperation I rang Bobby. 'You've got to take some responsibility,' I said. 'Dean's going off the rails. He's getting drunk and playing truant. I don't want to cope with this on my own. I *can't* cope with it on my own.'

Off Dean went to Southend for a fatherly talking-to. It was a disaster. Bobby might have realized he had to pull his weight, but he was still reeling from the shock of it all, too. With Dean, he did the worst thing he could have done. 'Now, come on, son,' he said, 'let's go and talk about it over a pint.' Dean returned barely able to stand up. Their relationship was bad for some time. Deep down, Dean was still enormously proud of Bobby but right now, he just didn't want to know his father.

Roberta was knocked off track by the split as well. She decided to go to Paris for a year to attend the Alliance Française while working as an au pair. I went over for a visit to make sure she was all right. She was fine but Mummy was not. As Roberta's host family were very chic, I had bought myself a Gucci handbag so as not to let the side down. The two of us went out to dinner and on the way back, strutting my stuff alongside the Bois de Boulogne with the bag swinging from my shoulder, I suddenly became aware of pounding feet and the sound of Roberta screaming out in French. Then I was pushed to the ground as a mugger ran off with my handbag.

'You stay there,' Roberta ordered, and ran after the

thief. She didn't catch him but came back with a *gendarme*. My evening out ended in hospital in St Germain, at three o'clock in the morning, with no money, no passport and no Gucci.

Roberta phoned Bobby to tell him what had happened and he wanted to fly out. That was typical of him. He hadn't stopped being thoughtful and protective. I suppose it was important to him to let me know he was still there for me, but suddenly I realized it was the last thing I needed. 'It isn't enough for me, Bobby,' I said. 'If I can't have all of you, I don't want any of you.'

It was a case of nothing being better than something. I was going to have to stop relying on him. I had let things slide long enough.

Turning my life around wasn't going to be easy. I had to wean myself off the sleeping pills. Then I had to get out of the habit of drinking at home on my own.

I wanted a job, too. It wasn't only that I needed the money. Self-respect was what I was looking for. But what work could I get? I had won a place at grammar school, so obviously I wasn't stupid. Even so, when I was in my teens, girls like me from ordinary backgrounds were less aspirational about education. As a matter of routine we were expected to leave school at 16, go to secretarial college, train as hairdressers or work in a shop until we found a husband. Only a few of my contemporaries would have contemplated staying on to do A-Levels and heading off to university before landing a high-powered job.

I wasn't one of them. When Bobby and I married, the expectation still was that unless a wife had to have a job to make ends meet, then she gave up work and became a full-time wife and mother. The husband and children were your universe. A husband's status depended on his being able to provide for his wife and family, which was one of the reasons why Bobby had felt so ashamed about his money problems. But when you split up from your husband, you're forced to take control of your own life. I decided the best thing was to give myself a target and challenge myself.

I had got a lot out of my seven years working for the Samaritans and for Roy, the sandalled social worker, so it made sense to put myself through college on a year-long advanced course in sociology and counselling. As part of the training I had to work with clients, so I found myself a placement at a clinic. Having a job to go to and making a success of client work began to restore my confidence.

By then I was already nerving myself for the final split. I no longer felt my heart leap when the phone rang in case it was Bobby. I stopped relying on him to come round and sort out anything that went wrong at home. One day, eighteen months after the split, we agreed to meet up for lunch. We went to Langan's, as usual.

'Bobby, I want a divorce,' I said.

That actually seemed to shock him. Perhaps he liked the fact that I was there in the background. I don't know. I just knew that I had to make him confront the reality.

'You know I'll always care for you, don't you?' he asked.

'And I'll always care too, Bobby, but you've turned my life upside down. I'm not going to live like this any more. We've got to make the break final. It's the only way either of us are going to be able to move on properly.'

'What are you going to do?' he said.

'I'm going to start a new chapter.'

I poured myself a glass of wine and walked all round Morlands. Bobby and I had always called it 'the home of our dreams' and reminders of the good times were everywhere. One of Rodney Marsh's fivers was probably still stuck in a hole in the grouting somewhere.

It hadn't been a happy house for a long time, though. I had set things in motion by telling Bobby I wanted a divorce. Bobby was unbelievably generous with the settlement – so much so that I cried and told him he couldn't afford it. Basically, he gave me everything and now Morlands had to go. I couldn't afford the upkeep.

DUE TO DIVORCE, ENTIRE CONTENTS OF LUXURY HOME IN CHIGWELL FOR SALE.

It was my friend Jill Budge's idea to put the advertisement in the *Evening Standard*. Word quickly got around that the home in question was Bobby Moore's and on the day of the sale a huge queue formed along Stradbroke Drive. All our friends rolled up. Once Bobby left, he effectively walked away from the Chigwell crowd, but I never felt excluded because of my new single status. Inevitably the sale turned into a party, with the usual moments of comedy. The local butcher was put in charge of catering but got paralytic instead and started groping all the girls. People were so keen to have a memento of Morlands that we were even cutting up the carpets and curtains. I thought I had got rid of everything, but at the last minute I glanced into the now empty lounge. 'Oh my God, I've forgotten Bobby,' I wailed.

Back in the halcyon days, we had been given a wonderful oil painting of Bobby by a prominent artist. There it was, hanging above the fireplace. We held a mock auction for it, but eventually I relented and it ended up going to Doss.

Wherever it was, my new house was going to be a lot less grand than Morlands. That was the first decision I made. I was very sensitive to the fact that Bobby felt he had failed financially and so we were no longer able to live the showbiz lifestyle – something I had told him time and again was of no importance to me. I was determined to downgrade as he had. Now I would prove the truth of my words to him, that I didn't need the high life. It was a case of, Anything you can do, I can and will do smaller. 'You were so wrong, Bobby,' I thought. 'I didn't need the finer things in life. You were what I wanted.'

I found a two-bedroomed house at King's Green, Loughton. It had a lovely location opposite the cricket ground and practically the first thing I did was to plant a magnolia tree in memory of the one Bobby and I planted at Glenwood Gardens, our first marital home which we had loved so much. I had overlooked one vital factor about my new house, though. 'Mum,' said Dean, 'it's only got two bedrooms.'

'Yes?'

'Well, when Roberta's home, that makes three of us. Who's going to sleep where?'

I was obviously still off my head when I bought it. I had forgotten I had kids! Whenever all of us were under the roof at once, someone had to sleep on a Put-u-Up in the front parlour, but the children refused to go in there because, they said, it was haunted.

I didn't believe that for a moment but even so, there was something quite unique about King's Green. It should have been called Queen's Green, really – every house bar one was occupied by a woman on her own. The token man was one half of a very nice married couple. He looked out for all of us ladies and was an expert at fixing the plumbing.

Our divorce went through at the start of 1986. My friend, Sue Braine, had split with her husband John just before Bobby and I broke up and she was heartbroken, too, but at least we had each other. It meant I had someone to go on holiday or spend a girls' day out in London with, so it wasn't all doom and gloom. Sue was like a sister to me and we did have fun, but she wasn't always available to go away on holiday with me. That meant that if I wanted to travel, I had to go solo. For someone who had been part of a couple all her adult life, it was one of the biggest challenges of all.

Geoff and Judith Hurst, who along with Alan and Lesley Ball were tremendously caring and supportive around this time, were going to Mexico for the 1986 World Cup and, knowing how much I longed to see Acapulco again, suggested I go to Mexico City with them and fly on from there. So I had two days with them before heading off to Acapulco on my own. I stayed in a suite in the Hyatt Regency. It had a colossal double bed which I rattled around in, and the next morning going to breakfast seemed a terrible ordeal. I wasn't used to it. I was lonely. But I did it.

Later, I started travelling alone further for longer. By then, Roberta had gone out to Australia and was so taken with the place, or possibly with Matt, the boy she had met while she was out there, that she was increasingly reluctant to return to England. I went out there to lure her back and took the opportunity to fly to the Great Barrier Reef. While there, I learnt to scuba dive. That would have frightened me out of my wits before. But scuba diving hadn't been my biggest fear. Loneliness was what really terrified me, but I made myself do these things to overcome my fears. It made me feel better about myself. I was healing, slowly.

For Bobby, meanwhile, the manager's job at Southend worked out no better than the others. In April 1986 he resigned and came back to London. There were no more management jobs on offer. Instead, he joined the *Sunday Sport* as a columnist. Dean joined the paper, too, in the graphics department, and from that point their relationship started to get better again.

Roberta was also back in London after her travels, working in event management for the Royal National Institute for the Blind. In October that year, she and Bobby were out at lunch together when he started feeling dizzy. He had chest pains, too. Roberta went with him in the ambulance to hospital. They suspected a heart attack. He sent a message to me via Roberta to say he would like to see me. I really wanted to see him, too. I didn't say so to Roberta, but if he was very ill it might be for the last time.

On the day I visited, I dressed up to the nines. It reminded me of going to see him in hospital when he was recovering after his operation for testicular cancer. I had been determined to look my best then and I felt the same twenty-four years down the line. This time it wasn't only that I wanted to look good for him. I was going to show the rest of the world I wasn't beaten.

Unfortunately, I felt so upset by the time I set off that my mascara was running down my face. I wiped it off as well as I could and then decided to buy him some strawberries. What I hadn't taken into account was that the weather was unseasonably hot, and during the journey to the hospital the sweltering heat turned them into a veritable blood bath.

When I reached Bobby's room, three people were already there: Doss, Roberta – and Stephanie.

I was formally introduced to her. We shook hands over Bobby as he lay in bed. Roberta told me afterwards that before I arrived, Doss had suggested to Stephanie that she leave Bobby and me on our own for a couple of minutes.

'I don't see why I should have to go anywhere,' Stephanie told her.

Poor man. The mother, the daughter, the girlfriend *and* the ex-wife. The room was fizzing with tension. I was very concerned because Bobby looked so on edge and the graph on the heart monitor was shooting up. I didn't want to finish him off completely so I took my leave quickly. But not before he turned to me and mouthed, 'You look lovely.'

I actually skipped out of the hospital. I knew he'd be all right. The problem had been diagnosed as hyperventilation – unpleasant and scary, but not life-threatening. As for me, I was relieved. I'd survived the meeting. I felt free – or at least, freer than I had been. I still loved him, there was no escaping from that, but I was feeling more like the old Tina.

* * *

Brief Encounter

Our paths didn't cross for more than two years after that. I carried on working as a counsellor. I had been offered a job at the clinic on a full-time professional basis, but to supplement my income I wanted to do something else a little lighter and more profitable. I had always really enjoyed hunting for houses and as bricks and mortar were the only things Bobby and I had ever made money on, I dabbled in property development and successfully 'did up' two flats.

Through our children, I knew that the *Sunday Sport* job had been a turning point for Bobby – the FA might have rejected him but the press never did and he was building up a successful media career. Capital Radio hired him to work as a co-commentator with Jonathan Pearce – he loved that work and was very fond of Jonathan. He was also involved in a new business, an event management group called Challenge, and Roberta joined him there. One of Bobby's staff told Roberta that he had worked for some really intolerable people, in contrast to which Bobby was the nicest employer ever. He had no attitude whatsoever – he would even make tea for the office staff.

Then one day, when I was on the Tube in rush hour, the oddest thing happened. A man sat down next to me and nudged me. Twice.

I threw him a cursory glance, but he didn't seem to be anyone I knew so I raised my eyebrows at the woman sitting opposite me and returned to ignoring my pushy neighbour.

I received a third nudge. 'Madam?' he said.

'What do you want?' I snapped.

The man laughed.

'Bobby!' I said.

That day I was wearing a cashmere coat. He reached out and stroked it.

'You always did like quality,' I teased.

I couldn't believe it. I hadn't recognized the man I'd spent twenty-five years of my life with. But I had always remembered him as the old Bobby – mischievous, gorgeous and laughing. This new Bobby looked gaunt, even haunted.

We talked until the train stopped at Bank, where he got off. But he hesitated and then, just as the doors were about to close, he jumped back on. We chatted and laughed about old times until my stop arrived, all too soon.

I rushed away, unable to get our meeting out of my mind. How did I feel? The same as Bobby, I suspect. I was talking to a reporter a while ago who told me that Bobby had mentioned our chance meeting. That touched me. Bobby was such a reserved, private man that he didn't normally open up to intimate and personal thoughts. The reporter had asked him how he had felt and Bobby had said, 'How do you think I would feel, walking away from someone I had spent half my life with?'

That was how I felt, too. I have thought of that meeting often. How strange that it should have happened at all, how odd that we had found each other when the train was so packed. There had been a spark between us but, then again, it's difficult to wipe out twenty-five years of highs and lows and not have any feelings towards the other partner. I had a knot in my stomach. It was because of the surprise of us meeting each other. No, he hadn't looked the way I'd remembered him, but one thing hadn't changed. He had always been such a shy man on the surface but his dry humour was still wonderful and I really, really missed it.

Roberta told me that he had called her that night, incredulous and amused that I hadn't known who he was. 'Only your mother could do that,' he said.

So in that way I hadn't changed, either. I could still make him laugh.

In the spring of 1991, I had a strange dream that really disturbed me. In it, I was wearing a dress that I recognized. It was a kind of pale lavender colour in real life, but in the dream it had turned dark purple. Someone had cut my shoulder length blonde hair and dyed it black. The dream was still vivid in my mind when I arrived at the clinic where I worked. I was convinced it was a premonition and that Bobby was seriously ill. 'I feel I'll never see him again,' I told a colleague.

At that very moment, the phone rang. It was Roberta, to tell me that Bobby was in hospital. It was just after his fiftieth birthday. She saw him in hospital the day before the operation. He was in a good mood, laughing away. The next day, after it was over, she visited him again. 'I think they got it all,' Bobby said. He was getting lots of laughs out of his drip, joking about taking it for a walk and similar. Roberta knew she wasn't being given the full story. She asked the consultant for the truth and he told her that a huge tumour had been found in the colon. The cancer had already spread to the liver.

After Bobby came out of hospital, he stayed at Jimmy Tarbuck's place in Marbella to rehabilitate for a few weeks. He went running every day. Back in England again, he was told the cancer was inoperable. To the children, he seemed philosophical. He didn't complain at all, just accepted it.

Or did he? Not long ago I spoke to Dr Kennedy, an old man now but one whose memories of Bobby are as sharp as ever. He told me that late one evening he received a phone call from Bobby, urgently asking his opinion about what could be done. Dr Kennedy agreed to see him the next morning at 8 o'clock and they spent twenty minutes discussing Bobby's failing health. It was the last time Dr Kennedy saw him. So it would appear that despite what everyone thought, Bobby was not ready just to give up. My heart went out to him when I heard this story and I realised how desperate he must have been. Right to the end he was fighting to beat this awful illness.

CHAPTER EIGHTEEN

Poppy Days

Dean and Sara had been childhood sweethearts. From when he was 11 until when he was 14, they went around everywhere together. Then they went their separate ways, as is the nature of things at that age. However, around the time he turned 18, the romance was on again. Over the next few years it turned into something more serious. They set up home together and in the fullness of time Poppy Grace Moore arrived in the world at just about midnight on 5 August 1991.

When Dean rang to pass on the good news I was in bed, but after I put the phone down there was no way I could get back to sleep. Instead I called Sue Braine and we both poured a glass of champagne to celebrate.

I went to the hospital, St Margaret's in Epping, at the earliest possible moment in the morning. I can hardly describe my feelings the moment I saw Poppy. I hadn't been prepared for them. They were so strong they nearly bowled me over. I was absolutely overwhelmed with love for her.

She had Dean's and Bobby's dimples and their lovely blond hair. Through Dean and Sara she was an extension of Bobby and me, and in the months that followed she was going to be terribly important.

That was because, just after Poppy was born, I left England for Miami. This time I wasn't going on holiday but to live and to work. I had a visa which was long enough to allow me to meet people and find out whether I liked it enough to make my stay permanent.

I'd been desperate to move away from the identity I'd had in England. There, it seemed impossible to escape from my past. I was fed up with people nudging each other when I walked into a place and overhearing them say, 'That's Bobby Moore's ex-wife.' I wanted to be judged for the person I was. There had to be more to my life than the fact that I had once been married to a famous footballer. I didn't want to hang on to Bobby's coat-tails. I wanted to become whole again.

Choosing Miami to re-launch my life hadn't been difficult. On holiday visits I had fallen in love with its cosmopolitan atmosphere and sunshine and seaside location. The Hispanic influence gave me a real buzz, so much so that I enrolled in Spanish classes.

What was tough was the utter loneliness and feeling of dislocation in my first weeks out there. I knew nobody, not a soul. I had gone over there completely cold and most of my friends in England thought I was crazy. Poppy's presence in the world helped me to get through. I discovered an outlet store where I could get designer baby clothes for a fraction of what they would have cost in England, and just being able to go out and buy her lovely things gave me a reason to go on and kept me mentally in contact with my family.

Christmas Day found me at my lowest ebb. To take my mind off the fact that it was the first time I had ever spent Christmas alone, I booked a tennis lesson at the club. I even managed to have fun. Then as we walked off court I wished Marco, my coach, a happy Christmas. Marco looked at me and said gently, 'I feel with you that although you're always laughing and smiling, you have a huge pain in your heart.'

His words just finished me. I ran back to my car. Blinded by tears, I headed for the end of the causeway. There across the water was downtown Miami. Its skyline was something I loved and had been one of the reasons I'd decided to live there. That, and the anonymity that now felt so desolate and painful.

'Tina,' I said out loud. 'You made the choice. Now get on with it.'

It wasn't just that I was incredibly lonely – I needed something in my life that was more substantial than playing tennis or golf all day. I was hungry for contact with other people, but I didn't want to go into the party whirl of

Miami or feel as if I was constantly on holiday. I wanted to forge a life and a living there. It was time to use the experience I'd had in the UK as a counsellor and a Samaritan. After looking up various help organizations and deciding I wanted something more hands-on than talking on the phone for a crisis line, I enquired at the local hospital in Coconut Grove. There I was offered work as a volunteer.

It was a great experience. I felt I was doing something of value and was giving a little back to the community. I derived a huge amount from it, too – making friends with other volunteers was just what I needed and with most of the hospital patients being Hispanic, I had to keep on with my Spanish classes and practise speaking the language whether I liked it or not. And like it I did. I stayed there for a long time. To support myself I did some paid work as well, but it was the Mercy Hospital that was my anchor.

By now I was settling down in Miami. My family and friends came to visit me and I got to know some of the local people. One, Peter Mansfield, was a big, colourful character who hailed originally from Stoke Newington in North London. We got on fantastically well – perhaps it wasn't just Bobby who was drawn to these larger-than-life types – and he offered me a job managing his photo and graphic design shop, Hot Shots.

Working at Hot Shots was great. At the time, Miami was a Mecca for modelling, with photo shoots happening everywhere. Peter had designed a new kind of Z card for models and we had all the top girls coming to the studio, including one very affected, pretentious girl who spent hours having her photos airbrushed to look perfect. She asked for 'White suit by Chanel' to be printed underneath one of the photos. Unfortunately, the person processing the order was from Colombia and she ended up with two thousand cards on which were printed 'White slut by Chanel'.

Meanwhile, I found a two-bedroomed apartment to live in. It was a flatshare and my flatmate was a charming and well-mannered young Englishman, Charles Afton, whose father had been the producer of 'Sunday Night at the London Palladium'. He worked, like me, at Hot Shots. The flatshare worked out very well in that Charles was often out very late, so I had my own space. On the other hand, at the end of those evenings out he would bring home girlfriends, of whom there were many – mainly young models. They would proceed to tell me of their hopes and aspirations and seemed to think of me as a surrogate mother.

At Hot Shots, Charles was in charge of the thirty-minute photo developing department, although I don't think the target of thirty minutes was ever achieved. All the photos and negatives were kept in a cabinet and when what Charles called a hot number turned up at the shop, he would open up the cabinet, produce wine, beers, cokes and glasses, then come round to the front of the cabinet and lean on it as if he was in a bar. The shop was also getting a lot of film work and one morning Peter and I were there together when the phone rang. Peter picked up the receiver, then said, 'It's for you.'

'Oh. Who is it, please?'

'Sean Connery,' Peter said.

'Oh, really.' He must be teasing me. I took the receiver from him.

'Hello, Tina,' came that lovely, deep, distinctive voice. 'I heard you were working at Hot Shots.'

'I can't believe it really is you,' I said. 'I'm just bowled over. It must be years since we met.'

We chatted about old times and I laughed when he reminded me of the time he had babysat Roberta and Dean in Marbella. I was tempted to tell him that Dean had become a father and that he and Sara would certainly appreciate his help with Poppy!

It was so good to hear from Sean. He had always rated very high in my estimation as a brilliantly successful man who nevertheless managed to remain astonishingly down to earth, and that day on the phone he was charm personified. Did I get brownie points for that phone call from Sean The Gorgeous!

After a few months, I returned to England. By then I knew that I liked Miami enough to make it my home and as soon as I could organize it I was on my way back and hunting for an apartment to buy. The one I felt drawn to was almost derelict but it was set in a unique position on an island on the bay and had the most amazing views. I decided to go for it. The next step was to get builders to make it habitable again. I hired a bunch of Nicaraguans – not the best policy as my Spanish was still quite limited. The first thing they did was pull the tiles off the roof, revealing huge, gaping holes. The second thing they did was decide the job was too much for them. They went off, leaving me in the lurch.

Inevitably, it was a really stressful period, but eventually I found someone I could trust to finish the job. As the place took shape I realized that what I had only dabbled in in England – buying old, dilapidated properties and refurbishing them – was truly my metier. I loved doing everything, from searching out the building to bargaining, renovation and interior decoration. I have done quite a few now, both in the States and in England, and I think I can say I've done A-OK out of it. I will be grateful to Miami for many things, and one of the most important is that it started me off properly in property development, which had only been an interesting hobby until then.

But most of all, I will be grateful, always, to Poppy for giving me that reason to go on in those first early months when I set off to discover myself.

CHAPTER NINETEEN

Is That Bobby Moore?

In autumn 1992 I went back to England for a short spell. I had had a phone call from Roberta, who said, 'There's no hope.'

Although I'd been aware that things were bad, Roberta's words still filled me with utter desolation. Almost the first thing I did when I arrived was to go to King's Green and put all Bobby's memorabilia in his England kitbag and send it round to him via Dean.

Some of my friends thought I was mad. 'Don't you dare send anything to him,' they said. But I wanted him to look at them one last time. I only thought of how precious they were to him and how much I wanted him to recall all those wonderful times and the honours he had achieved.

It was a desperately sad time. I already knew that Doss was also suffering from cancer. Dean had broken the news to me – Doss, typically, hadn't mentioned it. I felt for her. It had taken the two of us a while to establish a really warm relationship but she had always adored

Roberta and Dean, and when my mother died she was a real rock and we became very close. I was forgiven for 'taking her boy'.

Even after I went to the States, Doss and I never lost contact with each other. Knowing she was ill, I rang her once I was back in England. I wanted to see her while there was still time. At first she was 'feeling a bit under the weather' and wasn't up to seeing me. I felt a pang of hurt and rejection but no sooner had I put the phone down than it rang again. 'Come and see me this afternoon,' said Doss.

She was still living in the house in Waverley Gardens. I went there and we chatted about old times and I had my chance to tell her how grateful I was for everything she had done. 'I must have given you a hard time on occasions,' I said.

Doss looked at me and said, 'Come here.' She gave me a cuddle as she said, 'Tina, you've always had a big, big personality.'

I think she'd realized way back that we were both totally loyal to Bobby. We'd fought battles on his behalf. We'd never hear a bad word uttered about him. And because she said what she'd said with love and kindness, I took it as the ultimate compliment.

When it was time to leave, we kissed and hugged at the front door. We knew we'd never see each other again. Doss died not long after, thankfully before the son she loved so

277

much. But as I drove away from that place I felt at peace. Doss had absolved me.

After I travelled back to Miami, Dean followed me across the pond to join Bobby and Stephanie, who were having a last holiday at the Palm Beach Golf Club.

Dean had been a great support to Bobby during his illness, acting as his driver when he had to carry out his commentary work for Capital Radio. He spent a couple of days with him, playing golf, before he headed for Miami to keep me company. I was wobbling by then. We all were. On one of the days we spent together he and I went to a beautiful shopping mall, Bal Harbour, and had lunch. We ended up laughing and crying together as we remembered the lovely times we'd all had as a family.

'I know the break-up must have been dreadful for you,' I said. 'There was so much awful publicity, and you were only 14.'

'I felt very rejected at first,' he confessed. 'It was hard coming to terms with the fact he'd gone. That was why I went off the rails a bit.'

'I know how much Dad loves you,' I said, 'and Roberta too. He's really proud of both of you.'

'I know,' he said, 'and it's good that he and I have had the chance to become close again.'

I was devastated by what was happening to Bobby, but Dean got me through it. He was manly and reassuring, warm and caring. Whenever I looked at him, I was more and more struck by his resemblance to Bobby. It wasn't only the blond hair and dimples. It was in the way he leaned forward to look at you and listen intently. He had inherited Bobby's power to focus and for such a big young man, he was very sensitive and tuned in. You could see it in his softness with children. He was a joy to be with.

When Bobby left the States to go back to England, he must have known he was going never to return again. Dean followed him back and spent the last month of Bobby's life living at his home in Putney with Poppy. He and Roberta both loved their father very much. They knew they wouldn't have him for much longer and wanted to be there for him and with him.

Roberta asked me to tell this story, because it really brings home how much Bobby was loved by the public. Just before the news of his illness broke, she had been staying the weekend with Bobby. He told her he'd decided to put out a public announcement on Sunday evening because he was so visibly ill by then.

On Saturday, the day before the announcement, Roberta had gone downstairs to the kitchen where Bobby was doing his books, meticulous about everything to the last.

'I'm not working for Capital today,' he said, 'so why don't we go out of London for a nice lunch somewhere?'

They headed for Windsor and Eton, but by the time they

got there it was too late for lunch so they decided to go for tea at a hotel just over the river. Stephanie went on ahead to make sure the hotel was open while Roberta and Bobby waited for her on the bridge. Bobby was leaning over the parapet with his back to the road when a young lad came over. 'Is that Bobby Moore?' he asked Roberta.

Roberta started feeling very protective. Bobby was looking terribly ill and she was afraid the young lad would seem shocked. That would have upset Bobby. But she said, 'Yes,' and at that moment Bobby turned his head to look.

'Can I shake your hand?' the lad said. He was completely unfazed by Bobby's appearance.

Bobby didn't turn round completely, but reached over his shoulder. 'It's my pleasure,' he said, and shook the lad's hand.

The lad stood completely still for a moment, contemplating the encounter, then said, 'Do you know, I shall never forget that.' Then he walked off to join his friend, to show him the hand that had shaken Bobby Moore's.

Roberta almost ran after him to thank him. Bobby was looking so ill and yet the lad didn't see the illness. He just saw Bobby.

Bobby went public with his illness on 15 February 1993. It was the lead item on the early morning news. When Roberta travelled into work that day, everyone on the

Tube was reading about it. In the evening Bobby asked her, 'Did you see any of today's papers?'

'I didn't really feel like reading them all, Dad,' she said, 'but I went to the newsagent and had a quick look through.'

'Did any of them say anything detrimental?' he asked.

The modesty of the man! He was so unbelievably unassuming. 'No, no,' she said. 'They've said the most wonderful, wonderful things. How could they say otherwise?'

It's still hard to believe Bobby said that. It was astonishing that someone could be so unaffected by fame. He was so loved and admired and yet so unaware of it. He was only anxious that he hadn't let anyone down.

In the days leading up to his death, he had letters from all over the country. He might have been given the cold shoulder by the football establishment, but the rest of England knew what they were about to lose. They would mourn him with a passion.

I ended up sending two cards. I was in such a state of shock I didn't know if I'd sent the first one or not, so I bought another. I just so wanted it to be right. I didn't have to agonize over what to say. Everything was straight from the heart.

Bobby, I'm so sorry to hear of your illness. I want you to know my thoughts and prayers are with you and you'll always have a special place in my heart.

I might even have said, *I love you.*

Roberta phoned to tell me that a mountain of mail had arrived for him as soon as the news broke. He read my card, put it down, then picked it up again and showed it to her. 'That's lovely,' he said.

It gave me great comfort that I was able to tell him all this. That I could reassure him that whatever had happened, whatever he had done, it didn't matter. That's why I duplicated the card – I had to make sure he got it. I was just trying to say to him that all the harsh words and lies and tears and rows were of no consequence. I wanted him to be at peace and I wanted to be at peace with him because I knew I was saying goodbye. He knew what I meant.

Bobby worked right up to the last moment. His final commitment with Capital Gold was at the England game against San Marino. He was finishing his career at Wembley. He would have liked that. A couple of journalists rode with him in the lift on the way up to the commentary box. One of them said, 'We could do with you out there tonight, Bobby.'

'I think I might need a late fitness test,' Bobby said.

The cameras panned in on him in the commentary box. He sat there, gaunt, cap on. His voice was weak. When the game finished, he clenched his fists as if to say, 'I've done it.'

It was almost noble.

*   *   *

'Are you all right, lady?' said the cop.

'I'm fine, but someone I love is dying.'

The cop and his colleague had been standing on the sidewalk as I walked past, crying. I had been to the English pub in Miami. The intention had been to raise a glass of gin and tonic in Bobby's honour but I just couldn't do it. I pushed the glass to one side and gathered up my things. I just wanted to seek refuge in my apartment.

The cops were sweet. They drove me home. We had just got through the door when the phone rang. It was a friend, Sharon. She lived on her own. 'I've just fallen and damaged my ankle,' she told me. 'I can't move. What am I going to do?'

'Why don't you come over here where I can make sure you're OK?' I said.

Unbelievably, the cops said they would fetch her. They went over to her place, brought her back and helped her into the apartment, where I made up a bed for her. It kept my mind off what was happening in England.

Then I went to bed and fell into some kind of sleep. At five in the morning, the ringing phone woke me up. It was Roberta. She simply said, 'Dad died.'

I got dressed. Words can't describe how I felt. I wished I hadn't asked Sharon to come round. I just wanted to be on my own. I went for a long walk down to a church on Miami Beach. It was closed, so I stood outside and said a prayer for Bobby.

Over the days that followed, I wanted to lock myself away. My friends were kind, patient and generous. They would come and sit with me. I couldn't talk to them.

I could have gone back to England for his funeral but in the end I decided it would be the wrong thing to do. I didn't want my children to feel uncomfortable about my being there with Stephanie. So the day he was buried I went to church in Miami with a girlfriend and paid my respects to him there.

I was inconsolable. I couldn't stop crying. I don't know what I was crying over – everything, I suppose. Someone I loved had died. I'd had such wonderful times with him. He was so young when he died, the same age as my mother. He wouldn't see Poppy growing up into a beautiful young woman. Roberta would have children and he'd never meet them.

I cried for all the years that had gone. The beautiful boy who had asked me to dance. *Blue Moon, I saw you standing alone.* Me in my boat-necked dress.

Bobby with his first car. The red Ford Zephyr, paid for with the neatly bundled notes in the brown paper bag.

Bobby mounting the steps at Wembley on a summer's day in 1966. Carefully wiping his hand on the balustrade so as not to sully the Queen's immaculate glove.

Bobby holding up the World Cup, red shirt, sunlight on blond curls.

Bobby in Mexico, against Brazil. Bare-chested, swapping

shirts with Pele after the greatest game he ever played.

Bobby the father, cradling newborn Roberta in the crook of his arm. Running to Woodford Bridge on an Essex morning with little Dean on his bike beside him.

Bobby laughing, head tilted back. The man who loved life and lived it to the hilt.

And I felt he'd been cheated. He'd been so overlooked in his last years. He shouldn't have been photographed in his final days like that, when he looked so dreadfully ill. He looked so forlorn and brave and neglected by the football world. He shouldn't have died like that.

The last thing Dean did for Bobby was to brush his hair as he lay in his coffin. A strand had fallen to one side, and Dean knew how important appearance was to his father. At the funeral service he took him a red rose. On all the anniversaries that were important to Bobby and our family, he has done so ever since.

'Tina, it's Stephanie,' said the voice on the phone.

'Oh – hold on a minute, will you?' I went and fetched a glass of water. It wasn't that I was thirsty. I felt really taken aback and needed time to compose myself.

'They're having a memorial service,' she said when I picked up the phone again. 'The eyes of the press will be on us and I think we should present a united front and sit together.'

'Stephanie, I'm not going there to be seen,' I said. 'I'm

going there to pay my respects. I don't care where I sit. I'm not looking for public approval.'

I made my decision. I just truly wanted to be at Westminster Abbey on my own or with my loved ones. I didn't want any pretence on that day. I hadn't been to Bobby's funeral because I wanted my children to be able to think only about their father and not be worried or feel concerned about me. Now I wanted the same courtesy for myself, so I could say my farewells without any distractions to a man whom I had loved and who had been a major part of my life for twenty-five years.

And that, on the day, was what I did. I didn't expect or press the children to sit with me, but they chose to and I was so pleased they did. I felt as if Bobby was looking down and seeing all his loved ones, friends, team-mates and fans there, honouring him at this wonderful service in such a magnificent abbey, remembering him not only as one of the greatest footballers of all time but as a man who had touched the hearts and souls of so many. It was such an accolade. I savoured every moment.

CHAPTER TWENTY

Absent Fathers

I had been based in Miami for nearly three years when I started feeling restless again. Suddenly, the job at Hot Shots wasn't stretching me enough. I put it down to the process of self-discovery I was still going through. And it meant that when Roberta's SOS call came, it was perfectly timed.

By then Roberta was living in New York with Matt, who was working as a financial broker. She had been working as an events manager for *Irish America* magazine. Having had so much experience in that field from her work in London, the job suited her down to the ground and she was put in charge of a reception for Jean Kennedy Smith, Ambassador to Ireland, sister of Ted Kennedy and the magazine's Irish American of the Year.

Unluckily for Roberta, she was diagnosed with endometriosis during the build-up to the reception. It's a painful and debilitating illness and although, like the real trouper she is, she carried on working despite often being doubled up with pain, she found that the running around was too much for her. Mummy was summoned from Miami to give her a hand – or, in this case, legs.

The Tavern On The Green restaurant, a breathtaking and handsomely old-fashioned structure of linked conservatories in Central Park, was the venue for the Jean Kennedy Smith reception. We arranged for a podium to be set up for the awards ceremony, in which other prominent Irish Americans were also to be honoured.

Among Jean Kennedy Smith's achievements was her success in convincing the US Government that granting a visa to Gerry Adams would be helpful to the ongoing Northern Ireland peace process. Gerry Adams was a guest at the reception, as was John Bruton, the Prime Minister of the Irish Republic. It was probably the first time the two men had been in the same room and as well as generating enormous media attention, it entailed extremely tight security.

Pride of place on the podium was given to a specially commissioned Waterford Crystal sculpture that was to be presented to Jean Kennedy Smith. Three surgeons were also among those to be honoured and as they stepped onto the podium, one inadvertently allowed his sleeve to brush against the sculpture. There was a concerted gasp from the assembled guests, followed by a sound like a gunshot as the crystal hit the floor and shattered into hundreds of pieces.

The secret service went into a frenzy and the podium was suddenly surrounded by security men. Meanwhile, Roberta and I hurriedly found a replacement vase to present to Jean Kennedy Smith. Once the furore had abated, Donald Keogh, the former head of Coca-Cola, stepped forward to begin his presentation speech with the memorable words, 'Jean Kennedy Smith now has more pieces of Waterford Crystal than anyone else.'

Trish Harty, the co-founder and editor-in-chief of *Irish America*, was impressed with the work Roberta had done for her and suggested she set up her own PR and event management company. The idea appealed to Roberta, who invited proud Mama to be co-president. We called it RTM, the initials standing, of course, for Roberta and Tina Moore.

We were very lucky to have Trish behind us and organized a lot of events for her magazine. The one I am most proud of was a reception at the Plaza Hotel in New York to honour President Clinton, the following year's Irish American of the Year. It was a massive undertaking featuring captains of industry and A-list celebrities including Liam Neeson and Anjelica Huston, and involved working with the White House advance team. We were given a fascinating insight into what makes an event of that magnitude work and the White House team said Roberta was one of the best and most efficient event managers they had dealt with. They were particularly impressed with her dedication and eye for detail. I wonder where she got that from.

Bobby Moore

It was a once in a lifetime experience and wonderful to have the opportunity to meet so many interesting people, culminating with the President and Hillary Clinton themselves. One of my jobs was to co-ordinate security when they went walkabout at the end of the evening. I finished up having to form a human chain of hands to stop guests surging forward, especially one or two ladies with gleams in their eyes and their cards in their hands, ready to slip to Bill.

By then I had fallen in love with New York and decided to stay for longer. I already knew of a great place to live. A customer at Hot Shots had recommended the Teneyck, saying that it was safe and secure and for women only. It was also at a price I could afford, so without viewing it first, I booked myself in for a month.

What my contact at Hot Shots hadn't told me was that it was run by the Salvation Army. The first thing I saw as I stepped out of the cab with my belongings was its plaque, proudly displayed by the entrance. Inside was the familiar insignia of crossed flags either side of the doorway to the room where Vespers were held. I couldn't help laughing. 'I know Bobby's family were Sally Army people,' I thought, 'but never in a million years did I expect to end up joining them.'

The rooms were miniscule. Not that it mattered – I loved the quiet, comfortable Teneyck. Breakfast and dinner were

290

included, the location was fabulous, it was safe and secure and for professional women only, and the staff were some of the kindest people I'd met.

They did smile when I went out, though. Our PR business required us to attend a lot of upmarket venues, so I would gaily emerge from the Teneyck in my finery to a waiting limousine.

'Where you off to, girl?' the Teneyck doorman would ask.

'The Plaza.'

'Way to go, girl,' he would say, high fiving me.

I enjoyed my life in New York so much, the contrast between the modest charms of the Teneyck and the high-end circles I had to mix with on business. But my visit to New York wasn't only about relishing life again and starting to look forward to the future. Although I didn't realize straightaway, I was also on the brink of discovering something very important from the past.

My father's name was David Dean, so naturally he was known as Dixie. Virtually all I knew about him when I was growing up was that he was a businessman who came originally from Newcastle.

Now and then my mother and Nanny Wilde would let slip some tantalizing snippets of information, such as that he'd gone off with another woman and that she was Irish. I had a few shadowy memories of my own as well of

291

a tall, dark man once visiting our flat in Christchurch Road. I was around five or six at the time. What made his appearance stay in my mind was that he was carrying a wire-haired fox terrier puppy, which he gave to me.

I never saw the tall, dark man again. I had no idea who he was. For all I knew, he could have been my father. It wasn't something I would ever have asked. Any feelings of curiosity I might have had on that subject were quickly stifled by my loyalty to my mother. Whoever my father was, he had left her to bring me up on her own. As I've already explained, she had a tough time. She was beautiful and inspiring and deserved a better deal. Whatever the circumstances, and despite any questions I might have had, I wasn't going to betray her by seeking out the man who had caused all her heartache.

But that isn't the end of the story. I'm a bit reluctant to talk about this in case I sound crazy, but some years ago I went to see a clairvoyant. She told me I had a brother and sister. It was news to me.

What happened next was uncanny, an extraordinary sequence of events. In the summer of 1995 I had arranged to visit Ireland with Trish Harty in her role with *Irish America*. She and I had hit it off the moment we met and I knew I was in for a great time; as well as my accompanying Trish to various functions in her role with *Irish America*, we had booked a day out at The Curragh for the Irish Derby.

As Trish and I chatted on the plane over, the conversation must have turned to family because I remember half-jokingly saying to her, 'My father ran off with an Irish woman.'

'Why don't you try and find him while you've over here?' said Trish.

I laughed. I was still ambivalent about my father. The way I saw it, not only had he let my mother down – he had let me down, too. But the odd thing was that by the time the plane landed in Dublin, I found myself thinking seriously about what Trish had suggested.

After our day out at The Curragh, Trish refused to let me delay any longer. No sooner had we checked into the Mont Claire Hotel than I was whisked off to the bar. She found a seat and placed a Guinness in my hand. Then she disappeared. A few minutes later she returned with a phone book, open at the Ds. 'There are only a few Deans there,' she said. 'Please do it, Tina. I really think you'll regret it if you don't.'

She can be very persuasive, my friend.

Even so, I was really nervous when I started to leaf through that phone book. Cold-calling Irish strangers wasn't something I made a habit of doing. And in any case, what would happen if one of those Deans in the phone book really was my father? How would I feel if he didn't want to know about his long lost daughter? What if he rejected me?

293

But eventually I steeled myself to go through with it. Very tentatively, I dialled the first Dean in the directory. The number was answered by a man. 'Are you David Dean of Newcastle and England?' I asked shakily.

'I'm really sorry,' he said, 'but Mr Dean passed away twenty-five years ago.'

My heart lurched. 'Who are you?' I said.

'I'm his son.'

It was almost unbelievable – like scoring for England on your debut! I said, 'Well . . . are you sitting down? I'm your half-sister.'

'Ah,' he said. 'I know all about you. You're the one who married Bobby Moore.'

'How did you know about me?' I said, astonished.

'After my mother died, one of our relatives told us our father had previously been married to an Englishwoman and they'd had a daughter.'

What was more, not only did my half-brother have a family – he also had a younger sister. It was exactly as the clairvoyant had said it would be.

'How would you and your sister feel,' I said carefully, 'about meeting up now we've made contact with each other?'

'Oh, I think we should. How long are you over here for?'

'Only a couple of days. What about tomorrow?'

By now, Trish and I were both crying tears of happiness.

My half-brother and I arranged to meet at a bar and when I arrived there the next day, he and my half-sister were already waiting for me.

I felt an immediate bond with my half-brother and I think he felt similarly about me. He told me he picked me out the moment I walked in. I must have had a look of my father about me.

'Once, when I was very young,' he said, 'I was taken to see Ireland play England, which I thought at the time was a very strange thing for my father to do. He wasn't a big football fan at all.'

'Was Bobby playing?'

'Funny you should ask that,' smiled my half-brother. 'Yes. He must have wanted to see the man you'd married.'

So my father must have kept an eye on me from afar, somehow.

It was impossible to make up all the lost ground in one short meeting, but we decided we wanted to keep in touch and later my half-brother told me that the moment he met me he liked me. Even so, he did think at first that I was completely crackers because of the clairvoyant angle!

Meeting my half-brother and half-sister turned out to be a really healing experience. Although I had always avoided finding out more about my father, I had carried a lot of questions around with me throughout my life and they were able to supply me with some of the answers.

For instance, I'd always wanted to know why my parents

split up. My new siblings told me that during the war my father wasn't called up – he had an exemption because he was qualified to do underwater welding, a necessary and valuable skill in wartime. He was highly paid for it and travelled a lot. He obviously met the second Mrs Dean on his travels.

Their mother had been a glamorous blonde, like mine, while my half-sister was a pretty, voluptuous redhead. She found it hard to deal with me at first – I suppose she'd always been 'Daddy's girl' and here I was, a potential usurper. Happily, we got to be more at ease with each other as time passed.

They said my father had loved a drink and had been very charismatic. 'Whenever he was in a bar, he'd draw a crowd,' said my half-sister.

I laughed. Where had I heard that said of a man before? I was absolutely intrigued that although I had barely any memories of my father and he played no part at all in bringing me up, I had ended up marrying a man who in some respects sounded a very similar personality.

He died quite young of a heart attack, but he'd been a wonderful father to his second family. His first marriage, to my mother, had taken place when he was still young and finding his way in life.

So many gaps were being filled in at last, all out of one phone call. The uncanniest aspect was that because my half-brother's household had been receiving nuisance calls, they had arranged to have their phone cut off and a new, ex-directory line put in. The work had been scheduled to take place the day after I made that first call. If I had left it another few hours I would never have known my half-brother and sister, or been able to learn what kind of man my father was.

Finding out about him wasn't all sweetness and light. For a while I felt very angry. Why hadn't this wonderful man been so wonderful to me? I felt cheated that he hadn't bothered with me. But I wasn't upset for long. The next time I met my half-brother, he mentioned that our father had a lifelong love of wire-haired fox terriers and had bred them for many years. So that *had* been my father – the tall, dark man who came to Christchurch Road and gave me the puppy.

I travelled back from that later meeting thinking how life hadn't yet lost its capacity to astonish and amaze. I had been through huge events – divorce, moving to another country, Bobby's death. They had all played their part in my process of self-discovery. But it had taken a journey to Ireland and a phone call made almost on a whim to provide the final link in the chain – my father. I had wanted to feel whole again, and now I did.

Later that year, *The Times* Court and Social page was able to announce that *Roberta Christina Moore married Mathew Charles Hobbis on 28th October 1995 at the*

Chapel of the Most Excellent Order of the British Empire, in St Paul's Cathedral.

Getting married at the Chapel was an honour. It wasn't normally available to the general public, but Bobby's OBE, awarded to him for his contribution to football, made it possible.

Although Roberta and Matt had got together in Australia, the extraordinary thing was that they lived only twenty minutes' drive apart back in England.

He had been in the same football team as Dean when they were younger, and had met Bobby and me – in fact, the only Moore not to have met him before was Roberta. We both liked him and were delighted when he and Roberta got together. He was smart, intelligent and big-hearted and came from a sound, solid background. He even had the right pedigree. His grandfather, Harold Hobbis, played for Charlton Athletic in the Thirties and was capped twice for England, against Belgium and Austria. The Austria match was played in front of Adolf Hitler, who presented each of the team with an engraved silver lighter. During the war he had twenty-three games for West Ham. They included one on his wedding day: he left the reception to play, scored twice and returned to the wedding celebrations later that evening.

As soon as I met Matt, I could tell he would be good for Roberta in much the same way that my mother had recognized that Bobby would be good for me. Bobby had met Matt, too. Their first encounter was when Matt was 14 and hung out with Dean quite a lot. Later, when Matt and Roberta were going out together, they would go round to dinner in Putney with Bobby and Stephanie.

Having already spotted that Bobby was a compulsive tidier and arranger of objects, Matt would re-arrange the cutlery and cushions whenever Bobby left the room. Bobby was always puzzled when he returned to find everything in a different order from how he had left them. Matt was a prankster after his own heart and Bobby liked him a lot.

Roberta and I spent the day before the wedding together. After lunch at a nearby restaurant followed by the obligatory shopping, we booked into the Savoy and enjoyed dinner in the Grill Room: Dover sole, salad and one glass of champagne. Then we went to bed.

The bed was king size, so we shared. It was lovely to be with my girl and to give her a comforting cuddle. She was really upset about Bobby not being there – they had been so close. Finally, with the command, 'Mum, I must have a good night's rest, please don't make any noise,' she fell asleep. To be on the safe side, I stayed awake until I heard her breathing deeply.

All of a sudden I felt hot. Then sick. I dashed into the bathroom. Stricken with terrible food poisoning, I ended up lying on the marble floor while Roberta kept coming in to see how I was. It was four in the morning before we got any more sleep.

Our wake-up call came at seven o'clock. Poor Roberta was exhausted, but her name wasn't Moore for nothing. She got ready, had a glass of bubbly and looked like the original fairytale princess in her wedding dress.

Although Bobby wasn't there to give Roberta away, Dean filled the role admirably. As I watched them walking along the aisle, I thought how proud Bobby would be of them both. They had grown into the young woman and man Bobby and I always hoped they would be: Roberta is beautiful, elegant and, like the father she so loved and admired, cool and collected; Dean has inherited Bobby's shyness along with his good looks but, like his father, is at his best on the big occasions. He looked marvellous, filled with pride as he escorted his sister. They had turned out to be the most supportive, caring son and daughter and I just felt so lucky to have them.

So many of our friends and family were there and we all missed Bobby's presence acutely. He would have loved that day.

CHAPTER TWENTY-ONE

The Magnolia Tree

'Is that Stuart Higgins? I believe you've been trying to get hold of me.'

'Who's this?' said the editor of the *Sun*.

'Tina Moore. I'm calling from Florida.'

'Just a minute.' His chair squeaked as if he had swung round in it, and then I heard him shouting to the office. 'You'll never guess who I've got on the phone!'

'Jesus Christ?' someone asked helpfully. 'Elvis Presley?'

'It's Tina Moore!'

Loud cheers floated down the line and across the Atlantic to Florida. What I hadn't known was that Stuart Higgins and his staff on the *Sun* had been trying to get hold of me for weeks. They wanted to do a story about Bobby's World Cup medals. 'I've had people looking all over Florida for you,' he said.

Putting Bobby's memorabilia up for sale was big news, it seemed. I had done a lot of soul-searching about it. One hundred-and-eight full England caps; eight England

301

Under-23 caps; eighteen England Youth caps; one World Cup winner's medal; one European Cup-winners Cup medal; one FA Cup winners medal; England shirts, Pele's 1970 World Cup shirt. Over a twenty-one-year career of unsurpassed achievement, the memorabilia had piled up. When we lived in our first marital home in Glenwood Gardens, they had comfortably fitted on the plate rail in the lounge. By the time we got to Morlands, we had to have shelves and cabinets specially built to hold them.

After Bobby and I divorced in 1986, he gave me Morlands, its contents and all his football memorabilia. His attitude was that I had been with him when he had accomplished all his great achievements, so he insisted that he wanted me to have them.

He didn't just feel guilty about all the heartache he had caused me. He was also anguished and guilty about leaving the children. He told me that he wanted me to live as comfortably as possible. He also knew that I wasn't a fool and that I wouldn't squander his settlement. He knew that whatever happened, I would protect and care for all his medals and treasures and that ultimately everything, including the memorabilia or the proceeds from their sale, would pass on to Roberta and Dean and our grandchildren.

One of the most precious items was Pele's shirt, which is shown in the famous photograph of Bobby and Pele exchanging shirts after that great game between England

and Brazil in Guadalajara during Mexico 1970. Bobby had handed it over to Dean, who loved it so much that on some occasions he would sleep in it.

I had thought when I sent everything over to Bobby in that England kitbag that the Pele shirt from 1970 was there, together with some other England and swap shirts, but I was in such a state at the time that I didn't even know where I was, let alone exactly what I'd packed – much less thought about making an inventory. It took some time to get the memorabilia returned and what came back was itemized. I was on the point of returning to the States, so I just took everything to the bank for safe keeping.

It was only later, when I came back to England and went to check on everything at the bank, that I realized the Pele shirt and some of the others were not there. I have searched and enquired everywhere, but to no avail. It could be that in one of my moves from one place to the other they were lost or, worse, thrown away. I am just so sad and sorry that something Bobby had given to Dean and was treasured so much had gone missing. I can only hope that it is still in existence and that one day it will make its way back to Bobby's children and grandchildren.

It was around 1999 when I started thinking about selling the memorabilia. That came about because I sat down to work out my will. I began to realize how difficult it would be to divide everything fairly between the children. For a start, there was no way I could have given Bobby's World Cup medal to one rather than the other. That would really have caused conflict – the last thing Bobby would have wished. So I did the only thing that made sense to me and decided to offer the collection for sale.

My first port of call was the Professional Footballers Association. I told them what I was thinking of doing and they put me in touch with officials at a national football museum that was about to open in Preston. We agreed to discuss it further. However, I wasn't very happy with the casual way things seemed to be being handled and although in due course an offer was made, I turned it down. It wasn't enough but more importantly, it didn't feel right. Preston wasn't the right home.

Soon after, I was approached by collectors in Germany and Japan. News got around that I intended selling Bobby's medals and I was pilloried in some sections of the press. Bobby's memorabilia was the first from the Boys of '66 to go on the market, so perhaps the reaction was predictable. Even so, I was astonished when the story made front page news. The attitude seemed to be, 'How dare she sell it?'

What the press failed to acknowledge was that I had been pulling out all the stops to keep the collection together. It would have fetched two to three times what it did had I agreed to let the memorabilia be split up.

*　　*　　*

No wonder the *Sun* had been unable to track me down. By then I had been based in the States for eight years and, having lived in Miami and New York, I had decided to try out a new location. I had a friend who owned a mansion in West Palm Beach. It had had a triple detached garage that she had converted into a very pretty, typical Key West cottage, nestling in bougainvillea bushes and mango trees. It consisted of a kitchen, bathroom, sitting room and a bedroom reached by descending two steps. What my friend had not counted on was the Florida weather and once, during a really heavy tropical downpour, I woke up with the water lapping round the legs of the bed. However, it served its purpose. I discovered I preferred Miami.

It was Roberta who thought of getting in touch with Stuart Higgins of the *Sun*. She thought he might be willing to give us some more useful publicity about our fight to do the best thing by Bobby's memorabilia. She had worked with him before and thought he was a very straight sort of man. I went off to phone him, blithely unaware that all along Stuart had been devoting a considerable portion of the *Sun*'s budget trying to get hold of me.

I liked the vibes I got off Stuart. I didn't want this thing to be cheapened – and I didn't want the memorabilia to go too cheaply!

Stuart was very helpful. Like me, he wanted it to stay in England. The German and Japanese collectors who had approached me had mentioned astronomical sums of money, but England was where it belonged and West Ham was the most appropriate home for it.

Stuart introduced me to Tony Banks, then Minister of Sport, and suddenly the wheels were rolling. West Ham contacted me. So did Sothebys and Christies. Sothebys suggested splitting up the collection – they thought I would get more money. Then I spoke to Grant MacDougall, Christies' representative and a huge football fan. He felt the same as Roberta, Dean and me – that the memorabilia should stay together, in one place.

Negotiations opened. West Ham's offer was lower than that of the foreign bidders, but that wasn't important. My children were comfortable knowing that the collection would be intact and in a place where everyone could have access to it. We were all happy when it went to Upton Park. That was where it belonged.

What happened next was a comedy of errors. We had to make an inventory of the memorabilia, which I had kept in deposit boxes. By then they were stored in two old, battered suitcases in the vaults of the NatWest Bank in the Strand.

When the *Sun*'s representatives saw the suitcases, they fell about laughing and transferred the bounty into two smart new cases. With Grant MacDougall of Christies, Dean and I arrived at the Strand to start cataloguing everything. I promptly discovered I had brought the wrong keys to the cases. The right ones were still in the US. The bank manager produced a hacksaw and Grant got down on his knees and started sawing. When he managed to get the boxes open, he gazed in ecstasy at the treasures arrayed before him, pristine. Then he straightened up. 'The medals aren't there,' he said.

It was Oh-my-God time. You start doubting yourself. I knew I wouldn't have lost them. But where were they? Had I stored them separately, in some unusually obscure and even more burglar-proof cranny in the attic in King's Green? Suddenly I had a brainwave. 'They're with my personal jewellery,' I said. 'It's all in a safe deposit box in a bank in Loughton.'

Dean and I hopped onto the Tube to get them. We were about to encounter the next twist in the comedy of errors, although at the time it was anything but funny. When we reached Loughton, it was only to find that the bank wasn't there. It had closed down. At the time, my main bank was at Barkingside, so I put a call in there. They hadn't got the deposit box either.

A day of agony followed before I learnt that after closure of the original bank, the box had been transferred, unbeknown to me, and was at another branch of the bank at the other end of the High Street. Dean and I raced back to Loughton and took possession of the box. Predictably, I had no keys, so we jumped into a taxi and headed off to a locksmith two miles away in Woodford.

When the locksmith opened the box, I just couldn't help

myself. I picked up the World Cup winner's medal and held it before his eyes. 'Do you know what this is?' I breathed.

Dean and I bought another deposit box. We put the medals inside and took them over to the City of London Cemetery to show them to Bobby. It was a beautiful, early spring afternoon and right on top of Bobby's grave was a magnolia tree, just like the one he and I had planted in the garden of our first home. It was in full bloom.

We laid the deposit box on his grave. 'They're here, Bobby,' I said.

I just had to let him know that everything was there, intact.

Afterword

I was pleased, I can tell you, when the memorabilia were actually taken away and installed in the museum at West Ham. They were so precious to so many people and I had felt totally responsible for them. It was important that they stayed with the nation and West Ham have done a good job.

Now there is that big statue of him at Upton Park as well. It sounds ridiculous but whenever I go there, I sense his presence and it makes me cry. Not because I am still in love with him – that all finished long ago – but because I was married to this wonderful man for so long, and his children and I are so proud of his achievements. And I feel choked with sorrow as well. It is just so sad that he didn't live to enjoy his grandchildren.

Who knows about life? It could have been me dead and Bobby skipping about. Knowing that makes me determined to live every day as fully as I can. You never know what's waiting for you round the corner.

Bobby Moore

I feel as if my life has been charmed. I had a wonderful childhood, surrounded with love and blessed with a mother who cared enough to instill good values in me. I met and married a marvellous man. Over the twenty-five years I spent loving him and supporting him he gave me so much love, caring and fun in return. Thanks to him, I had a fantastic lifestyle and was able to meet some of the most fascinating people of my generation.

We had two children we both loved to distraction. They have inherited Bobby's tremendous strength of character and we have remained a close-knit family. I have three super grandchildren. Poppy is beautiful, elegant and loving. At thirteen, she has turned into a real stunner with thick, long blonde hair, beautiful thick-lashed blue eyes and dimples. And I love it that she has inherited Bobby's regal bearing.

Freddie, Roberta's first-born, came into this world on 28 April 1996 – he's a native New Yorker. The first time I saw him, I couldn't believe my eyes. I bent over his crib and kissed him and said, 'Oh – you're back!' I meant it. He was the image of Bobby.

His full name is Frederick Robert, of course, just as his grandfather was Robert Frederick. And like his grandfather he didn't like to sleep too much at first, especially at night. I was living in New York then, so I moved in with Matt and Roberta for two weeks to look after him. I was so happy when he and I bonded immediately. The best discovery was that I was the only one who could make him sleep. I would rock him and stomp up and down the room singing 'The Blaydon Races'. He loved it – or at least went to sleep to escape the racket. Now he has grown into a gorgeous, talented boy. Not only does he have Bobby's blond hair but, it would appear, his sporting ability – he is already rated a really promising tennis player.

And then there is Ava Elizabeth, Roberta and Matt's second. She was born, like Freddie, at Lennox Hill Hospital in New York. And the date? 30 July 1999 – the thirty-third anniversary of England's World Cup victory.

Once again I moved in with Roberta to help out and allow her to get some rest. Ava was a beautiful, sweet-natured delight from the start. She, too, has the Moore dimples, and curly hair like Shirley Temple's. She's a big, big personality, full of life and confidence – it's that X-factor which Bobby had. She lights up a room with her presence and her stunning smile. And me, 'Mimi', what do I think? I'm just madly in love with her!

But then again, I'm madly in love with them all. It's one of my great sorrows that Bobby isn't here to take part in their lives, but they love to listen to stories about him, not just of his fame and celebrity, but about Bobby the man and father. They always talk about Granddad Bobby. They will never forget him.

The end of my marriage was devastating. I never want to endure that sort of pain again. Even so, Bobby was right.

When we were splitting up, he told me that I was strong and that I would cope without him. At the time, I found that hard to believe but it turned out I did have an inner strength of which I hadn't been aware. I have discovered a very different person from the one I thought I was. I hope and believe I've grown as an individual through what happened to me.

I have made new friends on both sides of the Atlantic and worked hard to keep old friends, too. I value them all so much. They have helped me through the tough times and laughed with me at the many comic events that have come my way.

What has helped me all along the way is being able to laugh in adversity. That sense of humour is one of the things that attracted Bobby. As for my love of life, it hasn't diminished – it has grown. If I have learnt anything, it's that you have to 'grasp the moment'. *Carpe diem.* Some of the Latin at Ilford High did sink in after all!

I have made some decisions that seemed strange at the time and have taken many gambles. Fortunately, they seem to have paid off. I have gone into property development, both in London and in the States, and experienced the satisfaction of being successful at my chosen career.

The Argentine tango is one of my passions. I have got to know so many people through that wonderful dance. And having got so much enjoyment out of writing this book, I am trying my hand at a novel. My life is packed with friends and projects and activities and I have reached a stage where I feel contented and fulfilled.

Even so, I suspect I have many an adventure ahead – and I hope I have a lot of living left to do. Because part of me will always be that young girl in the boat-necked dress, stepping over the threshold of the Ilford Palais, full of anticipation and curiosity and with all the excitements and trials and joys of life before her. And like that young girl, I still believe that as long as you've got friends and money in your purse, you'll survive.

I am so grateful to Bobby. He has left fantastic memories that I treasure, and as I get older I realize how import-ant they are. Thank you, Bobby. You will always have a special place in my heart.

PHOTOGRAPHIC ACKNOWLEDGMENTS

The Publishers would like to thank the following
sources for supplying photographs:
Central Press/Getty Images 22cl; Mirrorpix 4t, 4bl, 11m, 11b, 12t,
18br, 19bl; Terry O'Neill/Hulton Archive/Getty Images 9 inset;
Topham 11t; Wesley/Keystone/Getty Images 18bl.

All other photographs provided courtesy of
Tina Moore, including the following:
Alan F Raymond 15t; Charlie Best 24b; Daily Express 12b, 14t;
Daily Mail 13t; Daily Mirror 6t, 6b, 7b, 16b, 17t, 19t, 20c, 20t;
Evening News 5b; Fotosports International 17c; Hatton 9;
John Adams Studios text page 326; Kent Gavin text page iii;
Keystone Press 10t, 16t; Picture Power 21tl; Press Association 6c,
8t, 12c, 14c; Sun 7t, 22tr; Sunday Mirror 22tl;
Syndication International 10b, 12b, 12cr.

*Every effort has been made to contact the copyright holders
of the photographs included in this book. Where there have been
omissions, the Publishers will endeavour to rectify any
outstanding permissions on publication.*

Index

Index

Index

Index

Index

Index